The TEXAS

Holiday Cookbook

The TEXAS

Holiday Cookbook

DOTTY GRIFFITH

TAYLOR TRADE PUBLISHING

Lanham ✳ New York ✳ Boulder ✳ Toronto ✳ Plymouth, UK

Published by Taylor Trade Publishing
An imprint of The Rowman & Littlefield Publishing Group, Inc.
4501 Forbes Boulevard, Suite 200, Lanham, Maryland 20706
www.rowman.com

10 Thornbury Road, Plymouth PL6 7PP, United Kingdom

Distributed by National Book Network

British Library Cataloguing in Publication Information Available

Library of Congress Cataloging-in-Publication Data
Griffith, Dotty.
   The Texas holiday cookbook / Dotty Griffith. — Second edition.
      pages cm
   Includes index.
      ISBN 978-1-58979-863-2 (cloth : alk. paper) — ISBN 978-1-58979-864-9
   (electronic) 1. Holiday cooking—Texas. 2. Cooking, American—Southwestern style.
   I. Title.
   TX739.G75 2013
   641.59764—dc23   2013020406

Printed in the United States of America

This book is dedicated to my brilliant and bold son and daughter,
Kelly Griffith Stephenson and Caitlin Lee Stephenson.
I love cooking and eating with them.

Contents

Acknowledgments

A lot can happen in 15 years.

Since this book was published in 1998, food and cooking have become as much entertainment as sustenance. Reality shows about restaurants, chefs, products, and culinary travel abound. Recipes are easily accessible online yet, somehow and in a big way, cookbooks continue to be in demand. It is the permanence of bound pages with stories, recipes, and luxuriant photographs that link our families and our culinary traditions. I dedicate this work to both change and continuity.

A Heartfelt Thank-You to:

Stephen Butt and Central Market for their appreciation of this book and for providing a carte blanche welcome to the ultimate Texas food market. No retailer has any better understanding of the Texas mystique when it comes to all things culinary.

Publisher Rick Rinehart, of Taylor Trade Publishing, for his visionary faith in this book and enthusiasm for the update; editor Karie Simpson for her diligence and sharp eye; Kalen Landow for her marketing; and Alden Perkins for her finishing touches.

Dedie Leahy, my friend and agent, for putting together the deal. Thank you for believing in me, encouraging, collaborating, and cheering me on. Working as art director, Dedie, along with her husband, photographer Rick Turner, have worked tirelessly to make this book a stunning visual reality. I owe them much.

Chef Stephan Pyles who wrote the foreword to this book. His understanding of and knowledge about Texas cuisine surpasses all understanding, and I am honored to have his generous words in this book.

Louise Griffeth for her generosity and gracious welcome to photograph in her beautiful home.

Betsy Moon, friend and colleague, for her good-spirited diligence and great assistance.

Elaine Corn, my longtime friend and a fellow cookbook author, for her brilliant ideas and indomitable spirit.

Food stylists Tonia Lyle, Martha Gooding, and Kris Ackerman, who made the recipes in the book look as appetizing as I intend the recipes to be.

Jeff Seigel, wine curmudgeon and founder of drinklocal.com, for his insight about wine, beer, and spirits in Texas.

Danny Sikora for his insightful consultation and elegant menorah.

Dedie's friend, Janet Watts, and my friend, Andrea Alcorn, for opening their cabinets and loaning us elegant pieces for photographs.

Foreword

Approximately 15 years ago when Dotty Griffith asked me to write a foreword to her now classic *Texas Holiday Cookbook*, I was honored. I said no other journalist in the state had done more to document the diversity of Texas cuisine and liberate it from its "barbecue-only" myth. I also said she had become the champion chronicler of our homegrown Southwestern cuisine, which captured the imagination of the entire country, if not the world. All that still rings true today. And with Dotty's 30-plus years experience in journalism and cookbook writing, she remains squarely at the forefront of the never-ending interest in Texas culture.

To see the extreme diversity in the cultural and ethnic influences in Texas cookery, one need look no further than the Texas holiday table. Throughout the years, that diversity has been transformed into a homogenous union that represents the very spirit of Texas.

Like me, Dotty is a native Texan, which means she has lived this book. It is her deeply rooted, multigenerational Texas heritage that gives this work its credibility. When she offers the reader a Thanksgiving menu of Roast Turkey, Texas Ambrosia, and Mole, it's not a menu that has been researched and developed but one that has been lovingly re-created based on years of tradition.

Reading the chapter on Christmas makes me nostalgic for the holiday foods of my childhood. Standing Rib Roast of Beef (cattle is king) was often paired with southern comfort food such as Cheese Grits. Where other than Texas would Roast Venison Backstrap (which suggests that Dotty had as many hunters in her family as I did) be appropriate with Cherry Cola Salad? I've been there—eaten that!

No chapter better represents the disparate but inclusive nature that is Texas than the one on Hanukkah. It reminds me of my Jewish childhood friends who taught me to celebrate and embrace diversity. It was also a means of discovering new foods, which has been an interest all my life. Latkes with Applesauce and Sweet Noodle Kugel will always have a place in my heart.

Dotty captures the essence of Texas in her menus for New Year's celebrations. Margaritas, Posole, and Migas set the tone of this fiesta while Brown Sugar–Baked Ham, Cheese Grits, and the obligatory Black-Eyed Peas bring a comfortable southern softness to the table. Finish the meal with Czech-inspired Kolaches, and the "big picture" of Texas cuisine begins to develop.

Since there's nothing more personal than a gift from hearth and home, the chapter on food gifts is alone worth the investment in this book. If you've never eaten or prepared the addictive southern delicacy Divinity, here's your chance.

Another major change in the culinary world of Texas is that there are dozens more talented chefs who are making names for themselves. Dotty has brilliantly added a chapter featuring some of our most gifted culinarians, their recipes, and a memory of some of their favorite holidays.

As with most other traditions in our great state, we Texans take our holidays very seriously. If indeed we are what we eat, it's no wonder Texans have such a spicy reputation. Dotty's *Texas Holiday Cookbook* is the perfect manual for bringing the fiery heart of Texas into your home for any holiday.

Stephan Pyles
Chef, author, and restaurateur

Introduction

Texans, Their Food, and Holidays

There are a great many sayings about Texas, but none captures the essence of the state any better than this one: Texas is a state of mind. And since this state has always been mine, I feel a special kinship to our people, our holidays, and, of course, our food.

What makes a Texan different from those who live in and love other states? To be Texan is to be proud. Being Texan is an identity to flaunt. To enhance. To nurture. To grow into. Being Texan supersedes other ways of thinking about oneself.

Tell someone you're from, say, Iowa. You get no visceral reaction. No sense of awe or fascination. Tell someone you're from Texas. You may get a reaction to stereotypes, but you sure get a reaction. No, not everyone in Texas rides a horse on the open range or drives a Suburban to count oil wells in the front yard. But, by golly, we can play the part.

Acting Texan is part pride, part bravado, part allegiance to a way of thinking, talking, even walking, and a way of feeling about yourself, your family, your land, and the image that goes with it. Texans like to say, "No brag, just fact." And we mean it.

Being Texan means embracing whatever cultural background you come from and melding it into the Texan way of doing things. Nothing illustrates this any better than serving tamales and turkey at Thanksgiving or preparing a Hanukkah menu of latkes and chili. That's unusual, even in Texas. But the combinations are understood and embraced.

Not that Texans are the same from the Red River to the Gulf of Mexico, the Rio Grande to the Sabine River. Panhandle Texans, accustomed to miles and miles of open prairie, are a different breed than the urban Texans of metropolitan Houston, Dallas, San Antonio, and Austin.

East Texans, with roots in the Old South and Cajun/Creole Louisiana, and West Texans, of the big ranch culture, are from the same state but with a lot of geography and customs in between.

Yet they're all Texan.

It strikes me as a testament to the Texas persona that someone from Kansas City, Missouri, for instance, might think of himself as an Irish Catholic from the Show-Me State until he moves to Texas. Transplanted, he suddenly becomes a Texan. No less Irish Catholic in family and religious-ethnic affiliation, but now a Texan.

It happens to newcomers all the time. Hence the bumper sticker: "I'm not from Texas, but I got here as fast as I could." And the proud rejoinder that simply reads: "Native Texan."

After all, Texas was once a nation unto itself. Understanding that the state once stood alone, then opted to join the Union, gives you a sense of the national pride that binds those who live within its vast borders.

When Texas was granted statehood in 1846, the annexation agreement included a clause that would allow the state to be divided into five states. But it can't ever happen. Texas then would just be another New England, a lot of small states with a regional identity.

If being Texan is a state of mind, Lone Star cuisine is a flavor and tradition all its own. It is not antebellum Southern. It is not Mexican, African American, or German, although all those flavors find their way into Texas dishes. It isn't rancho or hard-scrabble country cuisine.

It is Texas cuisine. No less an authority than nationally respected chef Stephan Pyles, a West Texas native of Big Spring, explains: Just as there're elements of Texas style in our clothing, homes, speech and outlook, "the Texas style has influenced the way people eat and cook."

That's why we were so pleased to partner with Central Market on the update of this cookbook. No one understands our state's culinary style and taste better than this Texas-born-and-bred specialty market.

Central Market has a true Texan's familiarity with the brash fusion of condiments, touches of flavor, and certain techniques that distinguish Texas food from others such as Southwestern cuisine, which reflects a lot of Hispanic, New Mexican, and Arizonan, as well as Texan, touches. Wonderful, but not pure Texan. That's why a Texas Christmas Eve might include sweet tamales, ham, cheese grits and rugelach.

Texas food has embraced the influences of the various ethnic groups that made the state their home. Now those influences are reflected in an amalgam called Texas cuisine.

Corn bread dressing was surely Southern in origin. Chili reflects the South Texas beef culture and the flavors of Mexico. Black-eyed peas for New Year's draws on Southern and African American influences. And barbecue, as practiced by the masters in the beautiful Texas Hill Country settled by Germans, shows how flavorful an old country love of sausages and smoked meats can be when adapted to a frontier with beef, some pork, hardwood, spices, and not much else. Of course, there are numerous other ethnic groups that have influenced Texas food—at least 30. And more are coming all the time as Texas welcomes new Texans from Africa, Asia, Central and South America, Eastern Europe, and the Middle East.

But the two types of food that are most frequently identified with Texas are Tex-Mex and Texas-style barbecue. Both types of cooking reflect Southern/African American, German, Hispanic, and cowboy ways. Jewish cuisine in Texas comes largely from the Ashkenazi traditions of Western and Eastern Europe and Russia.

Hence, the focus of this book is on the ways those ethnic traditions have come together to make up Texas cuisine, specifically the way Texans cook for the winter holidays, the most celebratory time of the year.

Starting with Thanksgiving, Texans cook up a storm until the last football game is played New Year's Day. There's no better reflection of a cuisine than the dishes that find their way to the table on seasonal holidays such as Hanukkah and Christmas.

Holiday cuisine, after all, reflects our best. The flavors on our plates are those we most love on our palates. Menus reflect traditions of the season, often common foods made special by ancestors struggling to build a new life. Menus also include foods often considered too expensive or hard to get except for a special occasion. Often, Texans salute their cultural heritage with a side dish, without which their holiday table wouldn't be complete. Tamales and roast beef on Christmas, for example. Special occasion meals reveal the touches that give a cuisine its identity: Southern-style corn bread dressing, not bread stuffing, for Thanksgiving; black-eyed peas with jalapeños for New Year's; Texas pecans in cakes, pies, cookies, on vegetables, in salad, and roasted for nibbling. These are the culinary traditions that give a home, a family, a state the identity reflected in a holiday menu.

Holidays may be the only time all year we use our best dishes, glasses, and silverware. Yet holidays aren't stuffy or formal for most Texans. Why not sit down to a holiday feast at a table set with Lenox china, Waterford crystal, and Gorham silver wearing cowboy boots and denim?

To understand someone's holiday cuisine is to understand their culture, their values, their heritage. To join someone for a holiday meal is to become a part of their family, to taste with their palate.

Come and eat at the Texas holiday table.

Thanksgiving

Thanksgiving begins the winter holiday season, a time for feasting, merriment, family, entertaining, giving, and, hopefully, some receiving.

But before all the other holidays begin, concentrate on the feasting. "I think Thanksgiving has always been my favorite holiday," says chef Stephan Pyles, a native Texan, well-known chef, and acclaimed cookbook author, "because the food was the main thing."

The native of Big Spring in West Texas has adapted his memories of regional favorites in his various cookbooks and the menus at his renowned Stampede 66 restaurant where he has contemporized traditional Texas cooking. He remembers feasts with turkey, enchiladas, stuffed jalapeño peppers, and the rest of the trimmings. "My family's table was derivative of West Texas, with its Mexican, Southern, and German influences," recalls Stephan.

Indeed, Thanksgiving is the most American of holidays, and it is the one where food is the symbol of the holiday. While Texans, like most other Americans, base their Thanksgiving traditions on the Pilgrim feast of thanks that took place in 1620, Texans can also look to their own history.

The documented Texas Thanksgiving, a meal shared by indigenous "Texans" and exploring Spaniards, is thought to have been celebrated circa 1598, which predated the more famous Massachusetts Thanksgiving by more than 20 years. Historians believe Indians and the Spanish explorers dined on turkey, venison, pumpkin, and corn together. Sounds a lot like the Chesapeake Bay menu, minus the oysters. And many contemporary Texas menus, for that matter.

Thanksgiving offers an excuse for a truly enjoyable, casual family party. In many families, everybody brings something. The day is wonderful for cooking, visiting, eating, visiting, cleaning up, visiting, and watching some football before everyone heads home and into full winter holiday mode.

THE CLASSIC
TEXAS
THANKSGIVING
MENU

Texas Turkey
(take your pick)

Roast Turkey, 10

Smoked Turkey, 11

Roast Wild Turkey, 12

Deep-Fried Turkey, 15

Corn Bread Dressing, 17

and Giblet Gravy, 19

Cranberry Sauce, 20

Really Whomped-Up
Mashed Potatoes with
Sour Cream and Cream
Cheese, 23

Candied Yams, 24

Green Bean Casserole, 21

Texas Ambrosia
(Fruit Salad), 31

Pecan Pie, 35

Pumpkin Pie, 37

My family's Thanksgiving was often spent on a hunting lease in South Texas, near the town of Pearsall. One year, we added rattlesnake to our holiday table. It happened like this. My dad (who his grandson, Kelly, persuaded us all should be known henceforth as Eddie Boy) was 'easin' on down' one of the rough, dusty ranch roads, flanked by cactus and mesquite, in his pickup. He heard a loud thump on the driver's side front tire. He threw on the brakes and jumped out to see what he'd hit.

What he saw, was what had hit him—actually had hit his truck. Lucky for him.

As he opened the door and stepped out, he was startled to see a rattlesnake, easily six feet long and three inches in diameter, strike the tire again.

Eddie Boy dispatched the snake with a shotgun. He brought the big rattler back to the camp house for all to see and shake their heads over the dozen rattles. Someone suggested, probably as a joke, that we have rattlesnake for Thanksgiving.

He took up the challenge. If butter and garlic can make snails taste good, why not rattlesnake? Eddie Boy flaked the white meat from the ribs and sautéed it in butter and garlic. It looked and tasted a lot like crab.

Although rattlesnake has never again graced our Thanksgiving table, that was one side dish we've never forgotten.

—*Dotty Griffith*

The Texas Turkey

In Texas, the most difficult part of the Thanksgiving meal is timing. It is common to plan the serving time based on kick-off time. The Dallas Cowboys have played on Thanksgiving Day for 40 or so years. And in recent years, the Houston Texans have taken snaps on Thanksgiving as well.

For many Texans, football is as much a part of the day as turkey and dressing. Some Texans like to eat before the game; others after.

The key is making sure that the turkey and everything that goes with it are ready at the same time. For that you need to know how long it will take to thaw the turkey, have a hurry-up method in mind (just in case), and calculate the roasting time. Try to do as much in advance as possible, so that all you have to cook on the big day is the turkey. Just about everything else should be a reheat or a last-step finish.

Texans are often on the move for Thanksgiving. If you draw turkey duty and you want to prepare it at home for taking to the host or hostess of the day, roast and carve it ahead of time. Store sliced turkey in refrigerator storage bags or ovenproof baking dish. Gently reheat in dish covered with foil at 300° until heated through (30 to 45 minutes) basting with a small amount of chicken or turkey stock to retain moisture. For a "turkey to go" recipe, see p. 230.

Roasting the turkey is the simplest part of the meal. Here's where I'll address the question, "To brine or not to brine?" Go for it if you like. I can't promise that you will think it was worth it. But I can tell you that brining a turkey takes time, refrigerator space, and some planning. Brining kits help. Frankly, I don't believe that brining makes or breaks a turkey. Thaw it. Put some oil on the skin. Roast it, basting now and then, and I think you'll enjoy your turkey and you'll be following the golden rule of enjoyable holiday cooking, KISS (keep it simple, stupid), wherever possible. The following techniques and recipes will put a turkey on your table. Go ahead and brine if you want but I don't.

Finding a bag of giblets in a roasted turkey has scared many a Thanksgiving cook. Don't be alarmed if you forget and bake the bag in the turkey. Just take it out and make sure there's no paper left inside the turkey. Proceed as if nothing happened. In this case, confession serves no purpose. It's not good for the soul, nor for the dinner guests.

TURKEY ROASTING GUIDE

POUNDS	HOURS
8–12	2–3¾
14–18	3¾–4½
18–20	4¼–4½
20–24	4½–5

Foil only protects the breast meat from drying if the shiny side is facing out because that side reflects the heat away from the bird. If the dull side was placed facing out it would absorb the heat and overcook the meat and make it dry.

—Tina Wasserman

Roast Turkey

1 (12–16-pound) turkey
2 teaspoons salt, or to taste
2 teaspoons pepper, or to taste
¼–½ cup vegetable oil
2 apples, optional
1 orange, optional
1 lemon, optional
2 fresh jalapeños, optional

Preheat oven to 325°. Rinse and dry turkey. Remove neck and giblet bag from the small cavity in the front, as well as the large body cavity. Use for stock (see Gravy, p. 19). Season inside turkey cavity with salt and pepper to taste. Use salt sparingly if using a prebasted turkey.

Rub exterior turkey skin generously with vegetable oil and place in a large roasting pan with shallow sides.

If desired, cut apples and orange into quarters. Cut lemon in half. Pierce jalapeños in several places with a fork. Insert apple, orange, lemon pieces, and jalapeños into cavity.

Roast turkey 15 to 20 minutes per pound. For most accurate gauge of doneness, use an instant-read meat thermometer. Temperature should read 180° when thermometer is inserted in thickest part of thigh. Juices should run clear when thigh is pierced at the thickest part, and the leg should move easily at the joint.

The turkey should be ready about an hour before dinner is served. Loosely tent with foil to keep warm, and carve just before serving.

Alternate seasonings instead of (or in combination with) fruit and jalapeño:

* Sprigs of fresh rosemary
* Bundle of parsley
* Fresh onion, quartered
* Sprigs of fresh thyme
* Sprigs of fresh sage

Serves 10 to 12, with lots of leftovers.

Smoked turkeys are probably second to roasted turkeys in popularity. Of course, cooks can smoke their own on a water smoker or covered grill, and the results will be delicious. But more turkeys are probably ordered smoked than are smoked at home. And for good reason. Excellent smoked turkeys are widely available: in supermarkets, from mail order sources, local caterers, or barbecue restaurants. Yet, there's something immensely satisfying about smoking your own big bird until it is mahogany in color, juicy and flavorful.

Smoked Turkey

1 (10–12-pound) turkey
2 cups pineapple juice
¼ cup soy sauce
2 tablespoons salt
3 tablespoons poultry seasoning
1 teaspoon dry mustard
1 tablespoon granulated garlic
2 tablespoons coarsely ground black pepper
1 tablespoon paprika
vegetable oil

Rinse and dry turkey. Remove neck and giblet bag from the small cavity in the front, as well as the large body cavity. Use for stock (see Gravy, p. 19). Place turkey in large reclosable plastic bag.

Combine pineapple juice and soy sauce. Pour inside cavity and over outside of turkey. Seal bag, squeezing out air. Turn bag several times to evenly coat turkey with pineapple marinade. Refrigerate several hours or overnight, turning occasionally.

Remove from refrigerator one hour before smoking. Drain marinade and discard. Combine salt, poultry seasoning, mustard, garlic, black pepper, and paprika. Sprinkle seasoning mix inside turkey, reserving some for the exterior surface. Lightly rub turkey with vegetable oil, then sprinkle with seasoning mix.

Meanwhile, prepare coals and cook turkey according to grill manufacturer's instructions. If using a water smoker, allow

The granddaddy of smoked turkeys in Texas is the famous Greenberg turkey from Tyler. Smoked almost black, these classic examples of deep-smoked flavor and rich meat are legendary throughout the state, nationally and internationally. If you want to try one of these classics, phone (903) 595-0725 or order online at www.gobblegobble.com.

approximately 1 hour per pound. Replenish charcoal as needed to maintain cooking temperature.

If using a charcoal grill with lid, light coals and allow them to cook down until covered with gray ash. Push coals against sides of smoker. Place a tray of water between the piles of hot coals. Place turkey on grid over the water tray and cover with grill lid. Cook 30 to 45 minutes per pound, adding additional hot coals as needed to maintain medium temperature.

Temperature should read 180° when thermometer is inserted in thickest part of thigh. Juices should run clear when thigh is pierced with a fork at the thickest part.

Serves 6 to 8 with leftovers.

It is a lucky hunter who has a wild turkey to grace his or her Thanksgiving table. These noble birds are prized for their wily ways and their flavor. While domestic turkeys are mild and juicy (some would say virtually tasteless), their wild cousins taste as distinctive as they appear. They do not have a "wild" flavor, rather a robust, meaty flavor, with herbal undertones. But like most wild game, the meat can be dry if it is overcooked. So take care.

When I prepare wild turkey, I test the breast meat for doneness. Often the legs are too lean and muscular to be enjoyable, so safeguard the white meat. If the legs and thighs aren't quite done and you want to finish cooking them, remove from the carcass and return to the oven for 15 minutes. Let rest along with the breast, then slice. Or, save them for the stockpot. Wild turkey does well in a roasting bag that will retain its full flavor.

My favorite Texas Thanksgiving sideboard holds platters of domestic and wild turkey.

Roast Wild Turkey

1 (8–10-pound) wild turkey or (3–4-pound) wild turkey breast
2 teaspoons salt, or to taste
2 teaspoons pepper, or to taste
1 apple
1 tangerine
1 jalapeño

3 tablespoons soft butter
2 tablespoons flour
1 large oven-roasting bag

Preheat oven to 350°. Rinse and dry turkey. Season inside cavity with salt and pepper. Cut apple and tangerine into quarters. Pierce jalapeño several times with a fork.

Follow package instructions for preparing bag for roasting. Make a paste by combining butter and flour. Rub over surface of turkey. Place turkey along with apple and tangerine pieces and jalapeño in roasting bag.

Roast according to package directions, or about 2 hours for whole turkey or 1¼ hours for breast, or until meat thermometer inserted in meatiest part of breast reaches 180°. When turkey is almost done, peel back bag and roast 5 minutes longer to crisp the skin. Reserve juices to pour over meat after it is sliced to keep it moist.

Discard fruit and peppers.

Makes 6 to 8 servings.

For a recent Thanksgiving feast, Sally Stephenson wanted to include wild turkey that her husband, Tom, had shot on one of his hunts. But she varied the theme, and made the kids, especially their son, Jack, who really isn't that crazy about roast turkey, VERY happy, with turkey nuggets, pieces of chicken-fried wild turkey breast meat.

Wild Turkey Nuggets

1 wild turkey breast, skinned and cut from the bone
1 cup buttermilk or as needed
2 cups flour
1 teaspoon salt, or to taste
1 teaspoon pepper, or to taste
vegetable oil for frying

Cut turkey breast meat into 2- or 3-bite pieces, about 2 × 2 inches. Place in plastic bag with buttermilk. Squeeze out the air and seal tightly. Refrigerate several hours or overnight.

Place turkey pieces in a colander and drain buttermilk. Dump flour into a large plastic bag; add salt and pepper. Close tightly and shake to combine.

Add turkey pieces, a few at a time, to flour and shake to coat. Remove from flour and set aside. Repeat until all turkey pieces are coated with flour.

Heat 2 inches of oil in a large skillet, preferably cast iron, over medium heat, about 350°. When oil is hot, add turkey pieces a few at a time. Do not crowd. Pieces should be able to float. Cook until golden on one side. Turn and cook until other side is golden, about 2–3 minutes per side.

Makes 4–6 servings.

Our neighbors in Louisiana get the credit for Cajun-fried turkey, but Texans have embraced this cooking method as if it had come from deep in the heart. All the ingredients are there to make a Texan love it: the cooking is done outdoors, it requires special equipment, the turkey cooks fast, and it is fried.

Actually, anything as big as a turkey doesn't exactly fry when immersed in hot oil; it boils. But the end result is a moist, tender bird with a golden skin. Done correctly, it is not greasy.

Like the smoked turkey, there are plenty of places to buy a Cajun-fried turkey in most major, and many minor, cities. But if you want to try it yourself, here's how. Just be careful. Fire departments all over the country report grease fires resulting from fried turkey experiments. Cook it outside, away from the house.

You'll need an outdoor cooker, usually gas powered, with a cooking pot large enough to hold 4 or 5 gallons of peanut oil and a turkey. Catalogs for outdoor equipment as well as hardware and camping stores often carry turkey-frying kits, worth the investment because they include lifters to make removing the turkey easier and safer.

There are also injector kits with syringes to shoot marinade into the turkey meat before frying. Otherwise, ample seasoning with salt and pepper, perhaps some cayenne, inside the turkey will do nicely.

This is a particularly good technique for wild turkey, because it keeps the lean meat very moist. As always with wild game, avoid overcooking. And don't let the scrawny appearance of the wild bird next to that plump domestic darling bother you. It doesn't look like a textbook turkey, but it tastes great.

Deep-Fried Turkey

1 (10–12-pound) turkey
2 teaspoons salt, or to taste
2 teaspoons pepper, or to taste
1 teaspoon cayenne pepper, or to taste
4–5 gallons peanut oil

Rinse and dry turkey. Remove neck and giblet bag from the small cavity in the front, as well as the large body cavity. Use for stock (see Gravy, p. 19).

Generously season inside cavity with salt and pepper. Be as generous with the cayenne as your taste buds allow. But don't hurt yourself; it's hot.

Heat oil in cooking pot large enough to submerse turkey in hot oil. For safety's sake, equipment for deep-frying outdoors is recommended.

Heat oil to 350°–375°. When oil is hot, using a sling of strong twine or string or a lifter that comes with a turkey-frying kit, lower turkey into hot oil. Cook about 5 minutes per pound or until meat thermometer inserted in thickest part of thigh reaches 180°.

Makes 10 to 12 servings.

For Wild Turkey: Prepare 4–5-pound wild turkey as above. Lower into hot oil and cook about 4 minutes per pound or until breast reaches 180°. Lean wild turkey will cook faster than a domestic bird. Don't overcook.

Makes 6 to 8 servings.

In Texas, it is dressing, not stuffing, and dressing is made from corn bread. End of discussion.

Some cooks may throw in some bread when they make dressing, but the traditional accompaniment to turkey is basically a corn bread mixture. The only question that may divide

Roast Turkey, p. 10, with Corn Bread Dressing, p. 17, (clockwise) Orange Asparagus, p. 27; Giblet Gravy, p. 19

some families is, "Wet or dry?" Sounds like a Tennessee barbecue rib feud, doesn't it?

Most corn bread dressing tends to be on the moist side, but there are some fans who like theirs quite crisp on top, with little croutons sprouting here and there. Often this type of dressing has chunks of white bread in it and always considerably less liquid.

D ressing is one of the Thanksgiving dishes you really should get a head start on. Bake your corn bread ahead of time. You'll need two batches for the dressing recipe.

Texas Corn Bread Dressing

12 cups Homemade Corn Bread (p. 18), or equal measure
   packaged corn bread stuffing mix
¼ cup butter
2 cups chopped onion
2½ cups chopped celery
1½ cups chopped, unpeeled apple, optional
¼ pound bulk sausage, cooked and drained, optional
2 eggs, well beaten, optional
5–6 cups (approximately) warm chicken or turkey stock
   (may use canned, or see Gravy, p. 19)
2 teaspoons salt, or to taste
1 teaspoon pepper, or to taste

P reheat oven to 325° or 350°. Lightly oil a 13 × 9-inch baking dish.

Place crumbled corn bread in a large bowl. Set aside. Heat butter in large skillet over medium heat. Add onion and celery and cook until vegetables are soft, about 10 minutes.

Add sautéed onion and celery to corn bread. Add other desired ingredients, such as apple, sausage, or eggs. The addition of eggs will produce a smoother, more custard-like consistency.

Toss to combine ingredients well. Add chicken stock and mix well. For moist dressing, the dressing should be thin enough to pour into the baking dish, quite moist, but not soupy. A small amount of liquid should collect at the edges. If there is too much dressing for 1 dish, oil a smaller baking dish for the remainder.

Place in oven during last 1 to 1½ hours before serving time. Dressing is done when it achieves a firm, scoopable consistency and the top is golden brown.

Makes 10 to 12 servings.

Dry Dressing: Substitute 6 cups bread stuffing croutons for half the corn bread. Use about 3 to 4 cups stock or just enough liquid for crumbly consistency. Omit eggs. Proceed as above.

Homemade Corn Bread

1¼ cups yellow cornmeal
¾ cup all-purpose flour, preferably unbleached
2 teaspoons baking powder
1½ tablespoons sugar
¾ teaspoon salt
1 egg, lightly beaten
2 tablespoons vegetable oil
1 cup milk

Preheat oven to 425°. Grease a 9 × 9-inch pan and heat in oven while mixing batter.

Stir together cornmeal, flour, baking powder, sugar, and salt in a large bowl. In small bowl, combine beaten egg, oil, and milk. Pour into cornmeal mixture and mix just to blend ingredients. Do not overbeat.

Remove pan from oven and pour batter into hot pan. Bake 20 to 25 minutes until edges are golden and pull away from sides of pan. The center should be set.

Makes 12 (3-inch square) servings.

My mother, Dorothy Griffith, was the queen of gravy. At her house on Thanksgiving, the turkey and dressing were really just an excuse to eat her giblet gravy. She had gravy making down to an easy science. Now Sally Stephenson has succeeded to the Thanksgiving gravy throne for our family Thanksgivings. Her gravy is reason enough to be thankful on the fourth Thursday of November.

Making the gravy unnerves many cooks. No wonder, if you save it to the very end when the turkey comes out of the oven and you're scrambling to get out the rest of the meal, hot, all at the same time.

One of Dorothy's tricks, however, has stood the test of time: Make the gravy ahead. Add defatted pan drippings if you like, when the turkey is done, but get the gravy out of the way a couple of days ahead. It'll just get better in the refrigerator. Don't plan on making it more than a couple of days in advance, especially if you're using giblets (chopped livers and gizzards).

HOW TO HARD-COOK EGGS

Place egg(s) in a saucepan and add enough cold water to cover. Place over medium heat and bring to a boil. Just when water boils vigorously, cover saucepan with lid and remove from heat. Allow to set, covered, for 18 minutes. Pour off hot water and rinse eggs in cold water until cool enough to handle. Peel under running water.

Dorothy's No-Fail Giblet Gravy

2 pounds chicken or turkey necks (or a combination)
1 pound chicken or turkey gizzards and hearts (or a combination)
9 cups water (divided use)
½ cup butter
½ cup vegetable oil
1 cup flour
3 teaspoons salt, or to taste
2 teaspoons pepper, or to taste
½ pound chicken or turkey livers (or a combination)
2 hard-cooked eggs, optional

Rinse chicken necks, gizzards, and hearts. Place in a large saucepan or stockpot. Cover with 8 cups water. Bring to a boil; reduce heat to simmer. Using a large spoon, skim off foam as it accumulates during cooking.

Cook until necks are soft and gizzards and hearts are tender, 2 to 3 hours.

Remove from heat and allow to cool. When cool enough to handle, strain stock into clean saucepan with lid or into a rigid plastic storage container. Refrigerate to congeal fat, several hours, up to 2 days. Freeze for longer storage.

Reserve gizzards and hearts; discard necks. Chop gizzards and hearts into ½-inch pieces. Refrigerate up to 2 days. Freeze for longer storage.

To make gravy, lift off congealed fat from stock and discard. Heat stock to liquefy; reserve.

In deep saucepan or stockpot, melt butter over medium heat. Add oil, then gradually stir in flour. Cook until flour is bubbly; reduce heat and cook until flour turns a rich brown, the color of cocoa.

Gradually add warm stock, stirring with a wire whisk to eliminate lumps. Cook until thickened to desired consistency, about 20 to 30 minutes. Season to taste with salt and pepper.

Meanwhile, rinse livers, if using, and place in small saucepan with 1 cup water over medium heat. Lower heat and simmer until livers are cooked through, 15 to 20 minutes. Remove from heat and let stand until cool. Drain livers and discard liquid. Chop livers into ¼-inch pieces.

Stir chopped gizzards, hearts, and livers into gravy. (See note below.) Add chopped hard-cooked eggs, if desired. Adjust seasoning as needed.

Gravy may be refrigerated for up to 2 days before serving. Reheat to serve. Thin with defatted pan juices from turkey or with water or stock to desired consistency.

Makes 16 servings.

Note: Not everyone likes giblet gravy. For those who want plain gravy, reserve some without the giblets.

⁓

My first recollection of cranberry sauce at Thanksgiving is the jellied variety. Slide it out of the can, slice it into rounds, then cut the rounds into wedges. It is still a staple on many Texas Thanksgiving Day tables. But fresh cranberries are more adaptable to Texas tastes. Although not native, the cranberry is something Texas cooks have taken to with enthusiasm. All sorts of native Texas ingredients—pecans, jalapeños, grapefruit, and wine—can make fresh cranberry sauce a Lone Star tradition.

Mix and match these variations to suit your taste.

Cranberry Sauce

2 cups water
2 cups sugar
4 cups (1 pound) cranberries

Combine water and sugar in a medium saucepan. Stir until sugar is dissolved. Bring liquid to a boil over medium-high heat.

Add cranberries and cook until berries pop, about 5 minutes. Skim off any foam that accumulates. Cool and refrigerate up to 1 month.

Makes 10 to 12 servings.

VARIATIONS

* ✳ Substitute ½ cup dry red or white wine for ½ cup of the water. Add to pan as above.
* ✳ Remove seeds and membranes from a small fresh jalapeño or small serrano pepper. (Wear rubber gloves and avoid touching lips, nose, or eyes after handling peppers.) Finely chop pepper and add 1 tablespoon or to taste along with cranberries. Add to pan as above.
* ✳ Grate 2 tablespoons peel from a Texas red grapefruit. Remove white pith and seeds from grapefruit sections and coarsely chop to measure 1 cup. Add along with cranberries. Add to pan as above.
* ✳ Stir in ½ cup chopped pecans after removing from heat.

If there is one dish almost as universal to Thanksgiving as turkey and dressing, it is green bean casserole. I grew up on my grandmother's, made resplendent for the holidays with the addition of slivered almonds. I confess I feel a little guilty about not creating a version of this classic substituting homemade mushroom cream sauce for canned soup but the more I thought about it, I decided not to. This version is traditional. If you want to modernize it, use fresh green beans.

Classic Green Bean Casserole

2 pounds (4 cups) fresh French green beans or
  1 (16-ounce) package frozen whole green beans
1 (10¾-ounce) can cream of mushroom soup
¾ cup milk
½ cup slivered almonds
1–2 tablespoons canned fried onion rings, optional

Preheat oven to 325°–350°. Cook fresh green beans in a large pot of salted boiling water until bright green in color and tender crisp, 2 to 3 minutes. Drain in colander and rinse with cold water to stop the cooking. If using frozen beans, place in colander and rinse with hot running water, or place in microwave, just long enough to thaw. Drain well.

Stir together soup and milk in a 2-cup measure. Place beans and almonds in large bowl and combine with soup mixture. Turn into a 2-quart baking dish. If desired, sprinkle top with fried onion rings. Place in oven and bake until top is brown and dish bubbles at the edges, about 20 to 30 minutes.

Makes 8 servings.

VARIATIONS

* Substitute grated Parmesan cheese for onion rings or other toppings.
* Substitute chopped toasted pecans for almonds.

Squash casserole, popularized in cafeterias and home-cooking restaurants, is a holiday tradition in many Texas homes. Ironically, it uses a summer squash.

Homestyle Squash Casserole

2 pounds yellow summer squash, about 4 cups chopped
2 tablespoons melted butter (divided use)
½ cup chopped onion
2 teaspoons sugar
1 teaspoon salt, or to taste
½ teaspoon pepper, or to taste
2 eggs, lightly beaten
½ cup cracker crumbs

Preheat oven to 325°–350°. Trim ends and coarsely chop squash to make about 4 cups. Place 2 cups water in a large saucepan and bring to a boil. Add squash and cook until squash is tender, about 4 minutes. Drain well. Place drained squash in a large mixing bowl and coarsely mash with a potato masher. Drain off any liquid that accumulates.

Combine 1 tablespoon melted butter and onion in saucepan over medium heat. Cook until onion is soft, about 5 minutes.

Add butter and onion to squash along with sugar, salt, and pepper. Stir in eggs.

Pour into 2-quart casserole lightly sprayed with nonstick spray. Sprinkle cracker crumbs over top and drizzle with remaining 1 tablespoon butter. Bake for 20 to 30 minutes until top is golden and edges are bubbly.

Makes 8 servings.

One Thanksgiving, dinner was on the table and we were ready to sit down when my mother asked where the potatoes were. Our whole family loves to cook and we'd all been in the kitchen, but somehow no one had made the mashed potatoes. So we all voted and decided that it would be better to put everything back in the kitchen and keep it warm while we made the potatoes.

—Mary Malouf

Really Whomped-Up Mashed Potatoes with Sour Cream and Cream Cheese

6 large (about 3 pounds) russet potatoes
¾–1¼ cups warm milk or half-and-half
1 (3-ounce) package cream cheese, at room temperature
4 tablespoons butter
½ cup sour cream
1 teaspoon salt, or to taste
½ teaspoon white pepper, or to taste

Preheat oven to 325°–350°. Peel potatoes and cut each into 6 or 8 chunks. Place in large saucepan with cold water. Water should just cover the potatoes when all are added. Cook over high heat until water boils, reduce heat slightly, and cook until potatoes are tender, about 15 minutes.

Drain well and return to saucepan over low heat, tossing well to cook away any remaining liquid. Using a masher or electric beater on low speed, mash potatoes, adding warm milk just until potatoes begin to take on creamy texture but before all lumps are gone.

Add cream cheese, butter, and sour cream, mashing or beating until potatoes are smooth. Stir in salt and pepper and adjust seasoning. Add more milk, if smoother, thinner potatoes are desired.

Place in 2-quart baking dish and bake until heated through and peaks turn brown, about 30 to 35 minutes. May be refrigerated 2 to 3 days before baking.

Makes 10 servings.

⁓

Sweet potatoes are another universal Thanksgiving tradition. Many Texans follow a Southern style and prepare canned yams with lots of butter, brown sugar, cinnamon, marshmallows, and pecans.

Candied Yams (Sweet Potatoes)

1 (29-ounce) can sweet potatoes, drained
1 cup chopped toasted pecans
1 cup brown sugar, packed
4 tablespoons butter, melted
1 cup mini-marshmallows

Preheat oven to 325°–350°. Lightly grease a 13 × 9-inch baking dish. Arrange sweet potatoes in bottom of dish. Sprinkle with pecans, brown sugar, butter, and marshmallows. Bake for 20 to 30 minutes until marshmallows are golden around edges.

Makes 8 to 10 servings.

⁓

The following version of sweet potatoes lets more of the naturally sweet flavor come through without so much gilding of the lily, to use an old Texas phrase. Roasting the potatoes, instead of boiling, caramelizes them and gives them a richer flavor.

Mashed Sweet Potatoes

6 (about 3 pounds) sweet potatoes, rinsed and scrubbed
1 cup brown sugar (divided use)
4 tablespoons butter
2 tablespoons bourbon or brandy
1 teaspoon salt, or to taste

Preheat oven to 450°. Lightly butter a 2-quart baking dish. Pierce sweet potatoes several times with a fork. Place in oven directly on rack and bake for 1 to 1½ hours or until they yield easily to the touch. Remove from oven and allow to cool slightly. Using oven mitts, cut sweet potatoes in half and scoop out pulp into a large mixing bowl.

Mash sweet potatoes using a potato masher or electric beater. Reserve 2 tablespoons brown sugar. Mix in remaining brown sugar, butter, bourbon or brandy, and salt, beating until potatoes are smooth. Spoon sweet potatoes into casserole dish.

Dish may be refrigerated at this point for 2 to 3 days before finishing.

Preheat oven to 325°–350°. Sprinkle remaining 2 tablespoons brown sugar over top of casserole. Bake for 30 to 35 minutes or until heated through.

Makes 10 to 12 servings.

⁓

This is a refreshingly new way to enjoy carrots. Mint butter gives them a different character.

Minted Carrots

1 (16-ounce) bag baby carrots
½ cup (1 stick) butter, melted
1 cup fresh mint leaves, lightly packed
¼ cup brown sugar, packed
1 teaspoon salt, or to taste

Preheat oven to 325°–350°. Place carrots in a large saucepan with enough cold water to cover. Cook over high heat until water boils. Reduce heat and simmer until carrots are easily pierced with a fork, about 6–8 minutes.

Drain carrots and place in a 1½-quart baking dish.

In a blender, combine butter, mint, brown sugar, and salt. Process until smooth and brown sugar dissolves. Pour over carrots and toss to coat vegetables evenly.

Place in oven just until heated through, 15 to 20 minutes. Makes 8 servings.

VARIATION

* Substitute 1 (16-ounce) package frozen green peas, cooked according to package directions. Drain peas and rinse in cold water to stop the cooking. Drain again. Return peas to saucepan. In a blender, combine butter, mint, 2 tablespoons granulated sugar (omit brown

sugar) and process until smooth and sugar is dissolved. Pour butter mixture over peas and heat through.

⁓

This simple treatment of asparagus, with a blend of sweet and savory flavors, is a refreshing addition to a Thanksgiving table.

Orange Asparagus

2 bunches asparagus
1 teaspoon salt, or to taste
½ cup butter
2 tablespoons finely grated orange peel
1 cup orange sections, cut into ½-inch pieces
⅓ cup grated Parmesan cheese or pomegranate seeds

If asparagus have thick, tough stalks, trim ends at point where stalks bend easily. Or, if stalks aren't too tough, simply trim the cut end and peel the bottom inch or so of the stalk using a potato peeler.

Cut asparagus into 1-inch lengths, starting from the tips. Pour enough water into a 12-inch skillet (not cast iron) to depth of 1 inch. Bring water to a boil over high heat and add asparagus and salt. When water returns to the boil, lower heat and simmer until stalks are easily pierced with a fork, but stalks retain considerable crispness, about 2 to 4 minutes.

Carefully drain asparagus so tips don't break. Rinse in cold water to stop the cooking. Wrap in damp paper towels and store in refrigerator until just before serving.

Melt butter in 12-inch skillet and stir in orange peel. Cook until bubbly. Add asparagus and orange pieces; toss to coat well. Cook just until asparagus are heated through.

Sprinkle with Parmesan cheese or pomegranate seeds just before serving.

Makes 8 servings.

⁓

Roasted zucchini have richer flavor than steamed or sautéed. You might learn to love this ubiquitous vegetable again.

Roasted Zucchini

2 pounds medium zucchini, about 6 squash
2 tablespoons olive oil
½ cup thinly sliced onion rings
1 tablespoon butter
1 teaspoon salt, or to taste
1 teaspoon pepper, or to taste
1 tablespoon finely chopped fresh thyme or 1 teaspoon
    dried thyme, optional

Preheat oven to 325°–350°. Trim ends of zucchini. Cut in half lengthwise. Cut each half into approximately 1½-inch pieces. Arrange zucchini in a single layer in a 9 × 13-inch baking dish.

Heat olive oil in a skillet over medium-high heat. Add onions and cook until onions are soft, about 3 to 4 minutes. Add butter and stir just until butter is melted. Add salt and pepper and thyme, if desired. Spread onions over zucchini pieces. Drizzle any remaining butter/oil mixture over zucchini. Toss to coat zucchini evenly. Add a bit more salt and pepper if desired.

Bake until zucchini and onions begin to brown on the edges, about 20 to 25 minutes. May be served warm or at room temperature.

Makes 8 servings.

Sally Stephenson found a way to make this dish for our shared daughter, Caitlin, when Birds Eye quit making frozen shoe-peg corn in butter sauce. We were all very glad.

Corn in Butter Sauce

2 (16 ounce) bags frozen white and yellow corn
2 teaspoons salt
½ cup butter
2 to 3 teaspoons agave or maple syrup
  (may use 1 to 2 teaspoons sugar)
1 cup water
1½ teaspoons cornstarch

Place corn in large saucepan with salt, butter, and syrup over medium heat. Stir until butter is melted. Combine water and cornstarch, stirring until cornstarch is dissolved. Slowly add cornstarch mixture to corn in saucepan, stirring constantly. Reduce heat to simmer and stir until sauce thickens. Let simmer, stirring occasionally, until corn is tender, about 10 minutes.

Makes 10 to 12 servings.

For many Texans, macaroni and cheese is traditional on a feasting table. Everybody's momma makes "the best." This version has a Tex-Mex touch with Pepper Jack (Monterey Jack cheese with red pepper flakes) and Mexican crema (similar to crème fraiche, thinner than sour cream). For a purist yellow cheese version, see Shortcuts chapter, p. 226, for a "no-boil" adaptation.

Corn in Butter Sauce, p. 28

Macaroni and Pepper Jack Cheese

1 pound elbow macaroni
3 tablespoons butter
1 small onion, chopped
1 small green (Anaheim) chile, seeded and chopped or
  1 (3-ounce) can chopped green chilies, drained
2 tablespoons all-purpose flour
1 cup milk
½ cup heavy cream or Mexican crema
2 cups shredded Pepper Jack cheese
salt and pepper to taste

Preheat oven to 350°. Grease a 1½-quart baking dish. Cook pasta to al dente following package instructions; drain and reserve.

Heat butter in a medium saucepan over medium heat. Add onion and chopped chilies; cook until onion is soft, about 5 minutes. Do not brown.

When onions are soft, whisk in flour and cook until bubbly, 2 to 3 minutes. Stir in milk, then cream and raise heat as needed to thicken the mixture, stirring constantly. When mixture bubbles and thickens, remove from heat and stir in cheese. Season to taste with salt and pepper.

Add pasta and stir to coat completely. If mixture seems too thick, thin slightly with additional cream or crema. Turn macaroni into prepared baking dish. Bake until brown and bubbly, 15 to 20 minutes.

Makes 6 servings.

Ambrosia is a traditional Southern touch for Texas holiday tables, from Thanksgiving to Christmas. Basically a fruit salad, ambrosia becomes holiday food with the addition of shredded coconut. This recipe is a guideline. Use whatever fruits you like.

Texas Ambrosia

Texas Ambrosia (Fruit Salad)

1 orange
1 grapefruit
1 red pear
1 green pear
1 cup seedless red grapes
1 cup seedless green grapes
1 cup cubed pineapple
1 pomegranate, seeded, or 1 cup pomegranate seeds
1 cup shredded coconut, optional
½ cup toasted pecans, optional
1 banana
1 tablespoon lemon juice

Peel orange and grapefruit. Be sure to remove the bitter white membrane called pith. Hold fruit over a large bowl while peeling to retain as much of the juice as possible. Slice the fruit into thin rounds. (This is much easier than trying to separate fruit into sections and it looks prettier.)

Core pears, but do not peel. Cut pears into eighths, then into bite-size pieces. Add to bowl and toss with orange and grapefruit slices, mixing well. The citrus juice will inhibit browning. (Apples may also be used, but they are more susceptible to browning than pears.)

If grapes are quite large, cut them in half; otherwise, add whole grapes to bowl, as well as pineapple.

No more than an hour before serving time, add pomegranate seeds, coconut, and pecans, if desired. Peel and slice banana. Add banana to salad and toss well to coat with juices to inhibit browning. Makes 10 to 12 servings.

Pies—particularly pumpkin and pecan—are symbolic of fall feasts. Relatively simple dishes, compared to the involved creations that make up the main part of the meal, these pies are nonetheless rich endings to an already sumptuous repast.

There's a cousin to pumpkin pie, however, that is just as traditional: the sweet potato pie. A standard in many Southern and African American homes, this delicious pie is similar in appearance but has its own subtle flavor, naturally sweeter than pumpkin. It is a wonderful Texas dish.

Of course, the easiest crust of all is cut and rolled for you, available in the refrigerator case at the supermarket. And there's absolutely no shame in using one.

If you want to try your hand at pastry, try this easy crust: simple to assemble and forgiving to work with. Not as flaky as a crust with butter or shortening, it nevertheless brings homemade crust within the reach of even a beginner.

Easy Pie Crust

1¼ cups sifted flour (sift before measuring)
¼ teaspoon salt
¼ cup milk
⅓ cup vegetable oil

Stir together flour and salt. Combine milk and oil; add all at once to flour. Using a fork, then your hands, combine flour and liquid to form a ball of dough. Flatten to a disk about 6 inches in diameter.

Press into a 9-inch pie plate, covering bottom and up the sides evenly. Crust should overlap edge of pan about ½ inch. Turn crust under and shape edge of crust using fingers to create a fluted or pleated edge.

An alternate technique: Place dough between two sheets of waxed paper. Roll the dough about 2 inches larger than the diameter of the pan. Remove top sheet of wax paper. Turn pan upside down in center of dough and, using edges of waxed paper, turn over both pan and dough to release dough into pie pan. Carefully ease dough into pan to fit the sides. Proceed as above.

Fill and bake as directed in pie recipe.

For a baked or "blind" crust, prick bottom and sides of crust with a fork. Place crust in 450° oven for 10 minutes or just until crust is set and begins to take on a golden cast. Cool before filling.

Makes 1 (9-inch) crust.

~

The following is a classic pastry. It works best with the pre-measured shortening, the kind that comes in wrapped sticks, like butter. This kind of shortening makes a flakier crust, similar to one made with lard, but without the cholesterol.

Basic Pie Crust

3 cups sifted flour (sift before measuring)
1 teaspoon salt
1¼ cups shortening (preferably premeasured in sticks)
8–10 tablespoons cold water

Sift together the flour and salt; using a pastry cutter, two knives, or fingers, blend shortening and flour mixture together until mixture is crumbly.

Stir in cold water, adding just enough for pastry to hold together, so that pastry forms a smooth ball.

If using a food processor, combine flour, salt, and shortening in work bowl. Process on and off several times until mixture is crumbly.

With motor running, add liquid in a steady stream and process just until mixture forms a ball.

Refrigerate an hour for easier handling. Divide dough and roll out on a lightly floured board to make pastry for a (9-inch) two-crust pie or two (9-inch) crusts. Roll the dough about 2 inches larger than the diameter of the pan. Drape crust over the rolling pin and ease it into the pan, fitting it against bottom and sides. Crust should overlap edge of pan about ½ inch. Turn crust under and shape edge using fingers to create a fluted or pleated edge.

Fill and bake as directed in pie recipe.

For a baked or "blind" crust, prick bottom and sides of crust with a fork. Place crust in 450° oven for 10 minutes or just until crust is set and begins to take on a golden cast. Cool before filling.

Makes one (9-inch) crust.

Pecans are a favorite all over Texas and you can find them in just about every course of a Texas holiday feast, from beginning to end. But these native nuts show best in a pie. Add a scoop of vanilla ice cream or a dollop of whipped cream and you've got a dessert to die for.

The following pecan pie is heavy on filling and nuts. Some pies go light on the filling so the pie is dense with nuts. I've always thought the custard was as good as the nuts.

We had been married six months; our first Thanksgiving together. We were working in Aspen. Without any of our Texas family to share the holiday with, lots of friends and coworkers were coming to our condo for the big feast. The night before, I decided I would make my first pecan pie ever. How hard could it be? We were playing bridge as it cooked and whoever was "dummy" would check the pie. It never seemed quite done; probably the altitude, we thought. Best we recall, it cooked for a couple of hours and we finally took it out of the oven. The next day when we tried to slice it, the knife went in and wouldn't come out. It was stuck. The guests were coming up the steps. Rushing to hide it, we threw it on a top shelf of the kitchen cabinet. And forgot about it. There it remained until we moved a year or so later. Still hard as a rock, with the knife still in it. I've never tried to cook a pecan pie since.

—*Terri Burke*

A pecan pie with beautifully arranged halves on the top looks pretty, but nicely chopped nuts in the filling make slicing easier.

Pecan Pie

½ cup sugar
¼ teaspoon salt
1 cup white or dark corn syrup
½ cup unsalted butter
3 eggs, beaten until foamy
2 teaspoons vanilla
2 cups coarsely chopped pecans or 1 cup coarsely chopped
   pecans and 1 cup pecan halves
1 unbaked (9-inch) pie shell, refrigerated

Preheat oven to 350°. Combine sugar, salt, and corn syrup in a small saucepan over medium heat. (Light or dark corn syrup will do. The flavor and color of the filling will be more intense and darker with dark corn syrup.) Cook until sugar dissolves and mixture is hot. Stir in butter and remove from heat.

Pecan Pie, p. 35

Stir until butter melts and liquid cools slightly. Add eggs, vanilla, and chopped pecans. Pour into chilled pie shell and smooth filling evenly. If using pecan halves, arrange on top of pie.

Make a ring out of aluminum foil to shield the crust. Place shiny side up over crust. Place pie in oven and bake for about 45 to 50 minutes or until a knife inserted in the filling comes out clean.

Serve warm with ice cream or at room temperature with a dollop of whipped cream.

Makes 8 servings.

Pumpkin Pie

1 cup canned pumpkin
1 cup evaporated (not sweetened condensed) milk
1 cup light brown sugar, firmly packed
3 eggs, lightly beaten
¼ cup bourbon or brandy
1 teaspoon pumpkin pie spice (or ¼ teaspoon nutmeg,
  ½ teaspoon ginger, ¼ teaspoon mace)
1 teaspoon cinnamon
½ teaspoon salt
1 (9-inch) pie shell, unbaked

Combine pumpkin, evaporated milk, and sugar in medium bowl, beating at low speed with electric mixer. Blend until sugar is dissolved and mixture is smooth. Stir in eggs, bourbon, spices, and salt. Mix well.

Pour filling into prepared pie shell. Bake for 50 to 55 minutes or until tip of a sharp knife inserted in center comes out clean. Cool on wire rack.

Makes 8 servings.

Sweet Potato Pie

2 cups canned yams or sweet potatoes,
  drained and mashed
2 eggs, well beaten
¾ cup milk
¼ cup butter, melted
1 cup sugar
1 teaspoon cinnamon
1 teaspoon vanilla
¼ teaspoon salt
1 (9-inch) pie shell, unbaked

Preheat oven to 350°. In a large bowl, combine mashed sweet potatoes, eggs, milk, and butter, mixing well. Stir in sugar, cinnamon, vanilla, and salt. Pour into pie shell and bake for 55 minutes to 1 hour, or until tip of a sharp knife inserted in center comes out clean. Cool on wire rack.

Makes 8 servings.

Shortcut Latkes, p. 232, and
Elaine's Applesauce, p. 49

Hanukkah

Hanukkah falls during the happy, busy time between Thanksgiving and New Year's. This is a special holiday for Jews everywhere, certainly no less in Texas. It is a fun holiday, particularly for children, who receive gifts each night of the celebration. The dreidel, a top, is spun for wagering, similar to the throwing of dice. Gelt, chocolate wrapped in gold foil to look like coins, is the currency of Hanukkah.

What, you wonder, makes a Texas Hanukkah? Oh, a combination like chile and latkes—not common, of course, but not unheard of in Texas. Christmas isn't the only season of blended culinary traditions.

As with other holidays in Texas, the spirit of the state influences the celebration. Jewish traditions have been part of the Lone Star State since before there was a Texas. The earliest Jews came from Sephardic (Spanish / North African / Israeli) communities with Spain's conquistadors. Later Jewish immigrants to Texas came mainly from Germany, Eastern Europe, and the Americas.

Hence the amalgam of traditions that characterizes the celebration of the eight-day Festival of Lights, commemorating the miracle of a single vessel of consecrated oil that burned for eight days. Foods fried in oil are symbolic of the holiday, particularly latkes (potato pancakes) and jelly doughnuts.

The holiday is observed by the lighting of candles, one for each night of the celebration, on the menorah, a nine-branched candlestick. The middle candle lights the others.

Jewish dietary laws as well as ethnic traditions set the menu. Since serving dairy and meat at the same meal isn't Kosher, a Hanukkah menu with brisket would include latkes garnished with applesauce, not sour cream. Recipes that call for butter may be made using margarine or oil as a substitute, but other dairy products, such as sour cream, cream cheese, or milk, are forbidden.

A dairy Hanukkah meal might consist of a variety of salads, such as tuna or chopped egg, various marinated fish dishes and spreads, perhaps a pasta or kugel (a noodle casserole), as well as latkes and sour cream. Jewish-style delis offer "dairy plates," a selection of dishes that adhere to Jewish tradition and dietary law.

HANUKKAH MENU

Chopped Liver, 40

with Rye or Pumpernickel Bread Rounds

Brisket Pot Roast with Vegetables and Gravy, 42

Latkes (Potato Pancakes), 45

with Elaine's Applesauce, 49

Savory Potato Kugel, 51

Fresh Spinach Salad with Texas Grapefruit, 89

Coconut Macaroons, 55

Old-Fashioned Sugar Cookies, 97 (omit dairy products)

DAIRY HANUKKAH MENU

Latkes (Potato Pancakes) with Sour Cream, 45

Dairy plate from favorite deli (egg salad or deviled eggs, tuna salad, herring in sour cream, etc.)

Texas Ambrosia (Fruit Salad), 31

Sufganiyot (Jelly Doughnuts), 52

Sweet Noodle Kugel, 50

Rugelach, 54 and Mini-Strudels, 57

You want to know about a Texas Hanukkah? Most Jews are pretty traditional, so there aren't that many new touches. But one time I sat down to a Hanukkah meal of chili and latkes. Now that's pure Texan.

—*Maryln Schwartz*

[author's note] My dear friend Maryln Schwartz passed away in 2011. We worked together at the Dallas Morning News for much of our journalism careers. She was an award-winning columnist and a best-selling author. She adored latkes.

Chopped liver is the punch line of many a Yiddish joke. It is also the beginning of many a Hanukkah feast.

Chopped Liver

1 pound calf's liver
3 slices white bread, crusts removed
2–3 tablespoons chicken fat or cooking oil, more or less as needed
4 hard-cooked eggs, peeled and chopped
1 teaspoon salt, or to taste
1 teaspoon pepper, or to taste
¼ cup finely chopped onion, optional

Preheat oven to 350°. Line a baking sheet with foil. Place liver on foil and bake for about 5 minutes. Turn and bake until cooked through, a total of 10 to 15 minutes. Juices should run clear.

Pull off skin; discard. Cut liver into chunks and place in work bowl of food processor fitted with chopping blade. Pulse on and off to chop to desired consistency. Add bread, then oil and process to desired consistency. Add eggs, salt, pepper, and onion; pulse several times to combine.

Chill and serve cold as a spread for rye or pumpernickel bread rounds.

Makes 10 to 12 servings.

Meatballs are a favorite party appetizer in Texas homes throughout the holidays. And they're a Hanukkah tradition.

Sweet-and-Sour Meatballs

1 (12-ounce) bottle chili sauce
1 (16-ounce) can cranberry sauce
3 pounds ground beef
¼ cup bread crumbs
3 eggs
3 tablespoons mustard
5 tablespoons ketchup
2 teaspoons salt, or to taste
1 teaspoon pepper, or to taste
1 cup water

Combine chili sauce and cranberry sauce in a large, heavy saucepan over medium heat. Bring to a boil, lower heat, and allow to simmer while shaping meatballs (or reheating prepared meatballs, turkey or beef).

Place ground beef, bread crumbs, eggs, mustard, ketchup, salt, and pepper in a large bowl. Using a wooden spoon and/or hands, mix well to evenly distribute ingredients. Add water to loosen mixture for easier mixing.

Form meatballs, about 1 inch in diameter. Add to simmering sauce mixture or transfer to slow cooker and cook slowly for 2 to 3 hours. Serve hot in a chafing dish or slow cooker.

Makes about 25 to 30 meatballs.

Pot roast has come to be a favorite main course for Hanukkah and brisket is the meat of choice. For Hanukkah, when there are already plenty of potatoes via latkes, consider substituting turnips or rutabaga for red potatoes with the pot roast. Or rely on the latkes for the starch factor.

Brisket Pot Roast with Vegetables and Gravy

1 (4–5-pound) beef brisket, trimmed of fat
2 teaspoons salt, or to taste
2 teaspoons black pepper, or to taste
nonstick cooking spray
2 cups thinly sliced onion rings, about 1 large onion
2 cloves garlic, crushed
1 cup water or ½ cup water plus ½ cup dry red wine
1 (8-ounce) can tomato sauce
8 medium red potatoes (about 2 pounds)
1 (8-ounce) package baby carrots
1–2 tablespoons instant dissolving flour, optional

Tip: For best results, use a flat cut or "first cut" brisket. This cut eliminates a fatty flap that can make for very greasy gravy. Be sure you buy a trimmed brisket, unlike for barbecue when an untrimmed brisket is preferable.

Rinse brisket and pat dry. Rub brisket on all sides with salt and pepper. Coat a large skillet with nonstick cooking spray and heat over medium-high heat. Add brisket and cook until brown on all sides, turning as needed.

Remove meat to a large platter to catch any juices. Cook sliced onions in pan drippings over medium-high heat until well browned and caramelized, about 10 minutes. Add garlic and cook just until garlic releases its fragrance, a minute or two. Remove onions and garlic from pan and reserve.

Place brisket and any accumulated juices in roasting pan and layer onions on top and all around.

Preheat oven to 300°.

Stir together water (or water and wine) and tomato sauce. Pour over brisket. Bring liquid to a boil over medium-high heat.

When liquid boils, cover pan with foil or lid and place in oven. Cook for 3 to 4 hours until brisket is tender. Check occasionally and add more water if the liquid evaporates.

When brisket is tender, remove the pan from the oven. Transfer brisket to a large platter; cover with foil and keep warm, reserving cooking liquid from roast.

Cut potatoes into quarters. Place carrots and potatoes in pot roast liquid and simmer over low heat, covered, about 15 minutes until potatoes and carrots can be pierced easily with a fork.

Brisket Pot Roast with
Vegetables and Gravy, 42;
Shortcut Latkes, 232, and
Elaine's Applesauce, 49;
Orange Asparagus with
pomegranate seeds, 27

Adjust seasoning with salt and pepper. If a thicker gravy is desired, sprinkle instant dissolving flour into gravy, stirring constantly. Cook over low heat just until thickened. Remove from heat and keep warm.

Slice brisket against the grain ¼ to ½ inch thick. Serve brisket with potatoes, carrots, and plenty of gravy.

Makes 8 to 10 servings.

VARIATION

* For a sweet-and-sour-style pot roast, add 2 tablespoons packed brown sugar and ¼ cup apple cider vinegar to cooking liquid. Omit red wine.

Roast chicken is another suitable Hanukkah entrée. This version uses mounds of dried fruit and almonds for stuffing.

Roast Chicken with Dried Fruit and Almonds

7 tablespoons olive oil (divided use)
3 pounds onions, thinly sliced (about 2¼ cups)
salt and pepper to taste
16 ounces dried apple rings
6 ounces pitted dates, halved
6 ounces pitted prunes, halved
10 ounces dried apricot halves
3 tablespoons sugar
1 teaspoon ground cinnamon
1½ cups chicken stock, additional as needed
2 whole chickens or 8 chicken quarters, thigh and leg attached, half breast with wing attached, or desired combination of pieces
1 teaspoon turmeric
1 teaspoon ground cardamom
½ cup blanched slivered almonds, toasted

Heat 6 tablespoons olive oil in heavy, large skillet over medium-high heat. Add onions and cook until deep golden brown, about 30 minutes; season with salt and pepper to taste. Stir in apples, dates, prunes, apricots, sugar, and cinnamon. Add chicken stock and allow mixture to come to a boil. Remove from heat. This step may be done ahead. Cover and store in refrigerator up to 2 days ahead.

Preheat oven to 350°F. Spread fruit mixture over bottom of large roasting pan. Arrange chickens or chicken pieces over fruit. Lightly brush chicken with remaining olive oil, sprinkle with turmeric and cardamom. Season to taste with salt and pepper.

Roast whole chickens for 60 minutes, chicken pieces for 45 minutes, checking periodically to see if fruit begins to dry out. Add chicken stock in small amounts to keep fruit moist. Continue to roast chickens until brown and juices run clear when thigh is pierced, about 15 minutes.

To serve, spoon fruit onto platter; top with chicken and any accumulated juices. Sprinkle with almonds.

Makes 8 servings.

I remember it as the night of the 80 latkes. I did not know how to make latkes ahead of time. I had not yet mastered the art of advanced preparation as my mother, Vivienne, had always done. I blended batch after batch of latke batter in a blender and made latkes for 2½ hours nonstop until all potatoes, matzo meal, and eggs and had been blended and fried in oil. The latkes were served with vats of sour cream, applesauce, and a variety of jams. There were no leftovers.

—*Elaine Corn*

The menu for Hanukkah is pretty flexible except for latkes. Jelly doughnuts are also a mainstay.

Latkes, more like hash brown potatoes than pancakes, may be served with sour cream or applesauce, depending on the rest of the menu.

A great latke is brown and crisp on the outside, white, soft, and steaming on the inside. The flavor and texture of a hot latke plays equally well against the cool of sour cream or apple-sauce. The former offers tart, creamy contrast, while the latter provides the palate with smooth, sweet refreshment.

Latkes (Potato Pancakes)

8 cups grated russet potatoes (peeled), about 4 large
1 cup grated onion, about 1 medium
4 eggs, lightly beaten
4 tablespoons matzo meal or flour
1 teaspoon salt, or to taste
½ teaspoon pepper, or to taste
vegetable oil for frying

Peel potatoes and place in a bowl of cold water to prevent discoloration. Fit food processor with coarse shredding disk. Feed potatoes through tube, emptying work bowl into a large colander after each potato is shredded. Shred onion and drain in colander.

Some cooks like to place shredded potatoes in a double thickness of cheesecloth or a coarse dish towel and squeeze to remove excess moisture. Don't fret if the potatoes turn pink, then start to brown. This happens when they are exposed to air. When cooked, however, they turn a lovely white-potato color again. You do want to work fast enough, however, to prevent them from turning the next shade, a dingy gray color. It won't hurt you, but that color doesn't cook away. Friend and cookbook author Tina Wasserman also advises that rinsing the potatoes under running water washes away excess starch and the discoloring culprit.

Using your hands, toss potatoes to combine with onions. Using your fingers, squeeze handfuls of potatoes or press potatoes into bottom and sides of colander to release excess liquid. Transfer drained potato and onion mixture to a large mixing bowl.

Add eggs, matzo or flour, salt, and pepper, mixing well to distribute ingredients and coat potatoes. Allow batter to rest for about 10 minutes.

Heat ¼ inch oil to 375°–400° in a large skillet. When oil is hot, but not smoking, drop batter by tablespoonfuls into hot oil. Batter will spread, but use the back of a spoon to flatten pancakes, if needed, for uniform thickness. Do not crowd the pan; the sides of pancakes should not touch.

Cook until brown on one side, about 4 minutes. Turn and brown other side, another 3 to 4 minutes. Drain on paper towels and keep warm while frying remaining batter. Serve immediately with sour cream or applesauce.

Makes 8 servings, about 24 latkes.

The following version of latkes is courtesy of Tina Wasserman. Also some more of her words of latke wisdom:

* Always grate your potatoes separately from your onions. That way you won't lose any of the flavorful juice when you drain the potatoes.
* The best way to drain fried foods is on a plate covered with crumpled paper towels. Crumpling gives more surface area for absorption.

Tina's Latkes (Potato Pancakes)

6–8 large thin-skinned potatoes, California long whites or Yukon Gold
1 large onion
3 eggs, beaten well
1 tablespoon salt
½ teaspoon freshly ground pepper
½ cup matzo or cracker meal
vegetable oil for frying

Grate the raw potatoes using the large grating disk on a processor or the largest holes on a grater if grating by hand. Place grated potato in a colander, rinse with cold water, and drain while you grate onion.

Combine eggs, salt, pepper, and matzo meal in a 3-quart bowl. Mix thoroughly. Change to the cutting blade on your processor. Add onions to the work bowl. Pulse on and off 5 times. Add ¼ of the grated potatoes to the onion and pulse on and off to make a coarse paste. Add to the egg mixture and stir to combine.

Add the drained potatoes to the bowl and mix thoroughly using a large spoon or your hands.

Heat a large frying pan or large skillet for 20 seconds. Add enough oil to cover the pan to a depth of ¼ inch and heat for an additional 20 seconds. Drop mounds of potato mixture into the pan. Fry on both sides until golden. Drain fried latkes on a platter covered with crumpled paper towels.

Makes 10 to 12 servings.

This variation, developed by Kyra Effren, uses sweet potatoes, definitely a Southern adaptation of the traditional Jewish favorite.

Sweet Potato Latkes

3 large sweet potatoes, about 2 pounds
2 onions, chopped fine
2 tablespoons flour
2 tablespoons rolled oats (uncooked oatmeal)
3 eggs, lightly beaten
1 teaspoon salt, or to taste
¼ teaspoon white pepper, or to taste
vegetable oil for frying

Peel the sweet potatoes and finely grate them. In large bowl, combine grated sweet potatoes, onions, flour, oats, eggs, salt, and pepper.

In a heavy-bottomed skillet, heat 1 inch oil over medium-high heat to 375°. Drop latkes by tablespoonfuls into the hot oil, flattening with the back of a spoon. Cook until brown on one side; turn and cook until brown.

Add more oil if needed during cooking. Repeat until all batter is used. Drain fried latkes on absorbent paper towels and keep warm until serving time.

Makes 8 servings.

Because my mother was from a Southern Baptist background and married a Jewish man, our holidays were always interfaith, to say the least. I remember when my mother took yardsticks and made them into a Star of David and put Christmas tree lights and tinsel on it.

—*Peggy Kligman*

Elaine Corn makes the special version of applesauce that follows. She recommends using just about any apple. You'll get great applesauce from Granny Smith, Fuji, Jonathan, Golden Delicious, Macintosh, Rome, or any combination. Red Delicious "is probably the least delicious in the entire apple kingdom," she warns. Her flavor enhancers—vanilla "to make it more like a pie" and butter "to make it rich"—take this applesauce to a new level. Elaine uses an immersion blender to make this an easier one-pot job. But any blender will do. So will a food processor.

Elaine's Applesauce

4 pounds (about 12) apples of any variety, to make about
  8 cups chopped
¼ cup honey or sugar, or a combination
2 (2-inch) pieces cinnamon stick
8 whole cloves (or 4 teaspoons powdered cloves)
¾–1 cup water
a pinch of freshly grated nutmeg
¼ teaspoon powdered ginger, optional
juice and finely grated peel from 1 lemon or 1 orange,
  or a combination
2 tablespoons butter
1–2 teaspoons vanilla, or to taste

Peel, core, and coarsely chop the apples. Combine apples, honey or sugar, cinnamon, and cloves in a large saucepan over low heat. Add just enough water to create a syrup to coat the fruit. Add a bit less water when using honey.

When liquid begins to bubble, reduce heat and simmer for about 40 minutes. Stir to coat the apples with the pan juices, then occasionally to prevent scorching. The apples will cook down to about half their original volume and become very soft.

Remove cinnamon stick and whole cloves. If a smooth applesauce is desired, process directly in the pot with an immersible blender until very smooth, or process in batches until smooth in a blender. Do not process if a chunky applesauce is desired.

Reheat applesauce over low heat, adding nutmeg, ginger, lemon or orange juice, and grated peel. Simmer until heated through. Remove from heat and stir in butter and vanilla to taste.

Makes 10 to 12 servings.

Kugels, noodle or potato puddings, can be sweet with fruit or savory with onion, with or without dairy. Nondairy kugels are served as side dishes with meat meals. Dairy kugels, sweet or savory, may be served as meatless entrées or side dishes, like macaroni and cheese, or as desserts. Traditional for holiday meals, kugels are as varied as the families who make them. Here are sweet and savory varieties.

Sweet Noodle Kugel

8 ounces wide egg noodles

1 (8-ounce) package cream cheese, softened, or cottage cheese

½ cup butter, softened

4 eggs

1 cup milk

¾ cup sugar

1 teaspoon vanilla

2 cups cornflakes, optional

1 teaspoon cinnamon or nutmeg

Preheat oven to 350°. Grease or butter a 9 × 13-inch glass baking dish or two 8 × 8-inch baking dishes.

Cook noodles according to package directions. Drain noodles and set aside.

In a medium bowl, combine cream cheese or cottage cheese, butter, eggs, milk, sugar, and vanilla. Using an electric mixer, beat on medium speed until mixture is well blended and smooth.

Pour cheese mixture over noodles. If desired, top with cornflakes. Sprinkle with cinnamon or nutmeg. Bake for 45 minutes or until golden on top and custard is set.

Makes 4 to 6 servings.

VARIATION

* For a savory noodle kugel, substitute 2 cups sour cream for milk and stir in 1 teaspoon salt, or to taste, and 1 teaspoon pepper. Omit sugar and vanilla; cornflakes are optional. Sprinkle with nutmeg.

Savory Potato Kugel

8 cups grated russet potato (peeled), about 4 large
1 cup grated onion, about 1 medium
4 eggs, slightly beaten
1 teaspoon salt, or to taste
1 teaspoon pepper, or to taste
5–6 tablespoons vegetable oil or chicken fat

Brush a 9 × 13-inch glass baking dish with oil or spray generously with nonstick spray. Preheat oven to 350°.

Peel potatoes and place in a bowl of cold water to prevent discoloration. Grate potatoes using shredding blade of food processor. Feed potatoes through tube, one at a time. Empty potatoes into a colander to drain. Repeat until each potato is shredded. When all potatoes are shredded, remove shredding disk and attach blade. Chop onion, using on-off pulses. Place chopped onion in colander with potatoes. Press with the back of a spoon to squeeze out excess liquid. Stir and repeat several times. Transfer shredded potatoes into a large mixing bowl.

Stir in eggs, salt, pepper, and oil. Mix well to coat potato and stop discoloration. Pour into prepared dish and bake for approximately 1 hour. Raise oven temperature to 450° and bake 5 to 10 minutes longer, or until top is browned.

Makes 8 to 10 servings.

VARIATIONS

* Cook 16 ounces dry noodles according to package directions. Substitute for grated potato and prepare as above.
* If desired, sprinkle with 1 cup crushed cornflakes before baking.

Jelly doughnuts, called *Sufganiyot*, are an Israeli tradition, most likely modified by European preferences. While the fried dough is considered Middle Eastern, the jelly filling is attributed to European immigrants, probably German. At any rate, these treats fill the Hanukkah bill since they are fried in oil.

Tip: For the true flavor of Jewish cuisine, use schmaltz—chicken fat—instead of vegetable oil. Of course, concern about fat—it is laden with cholesterol—causes many people to cook with oil instead. But for authentic flavor, splurge on the real thing.

Sufganiyot (Jelly Doughnuts)

2 envelopes dry yeast
4 tablespoons sugar (divided use)
¾ cup lukewarm milk
2 egg yolks
1½ tablespoons margarine, softened at room temperature
½ teaspoon salt
2½ cups all-purpose flour, sifted
vegetable oil for deep-frying
1 (20-ounce) jar grape jelly, or apricot or strawberry jam
1½ cups granulated sugar or confectioners' sugar

Dissolve yeast and 2 tablespoons sugar in warm milk. Stir and let sit until bubbly, about 5 minutes.

In large mixing bowl, combine egg yolks and margarine. Stir in milk mixture and remaining 2 tablespoons sugar, beating well. Sift together salt and flour. Gradually add sifted flour to milk mixture, stirring after each addition, to make a workable dough.

Turn out dough onto a lightly floured board and knead until smooth, about 10 minutes. Lightly rub another large, clean bowl with shortening or margarine. Place dough in bowl, cover, and let rise in a warm place, 2 to 2½ hours.

After first rise, turn out dough onto a lightly floured board and knead a couple of times. Let rest about 10 minutes, then roll thin, to about ½-inch thickness. Cut into 2-inch rounds. Remove scraps. Cover rounds and let rise 15 minutes or more, until doubled in size. Roll again and cut remaining dough into rounds.

Heat about 2 to 3 inches oil in a deep-sided pan to 375°. Drop doughnuts, a few at a time, turning once, and fry until golden, 2 to 3 minutes on each side. Be careful not to overcook. The dough will puff when it hits the hot oil. Drain briefly on absorbent paper towels.

Using a tiny spoon, insert a small spoonful of jelly or jam in the top or side of the doughnut. Twirl spoon to release filling and carefully remove spoon through the same hole. Thumbs and fingers are helpful here, too. Roll doughnut in granulated sugar or dust tops with confectioners' sugar. Serve warm.

Makes about 2 dozen.

Elaine Corn shared her mother Vivienne's recipe for this Hanukkah favorite. Chocolate chips are optional but a great add-in.

Doughnut (Sufganiyot) Drops

2 eggs
¼ cup sugar
1 teaspoon salt
2 tablespoons melted butter
1½ cups flour
4 teaspoons baking powder
½ cup milk
1 (6-ounce) package chocolate chips, optional
vegetable oil for frying

Place eggs in a large bowl and beat until light yellow and slightly thickened. Add sugar, salt, and butter. Combine flour and baking powder.

Add flour mixture and milk, alternately, to eggs, mixing well after each addition. Stir in chocolate chips, if desired.

Heat 2 to 3 inches of oil in a deep-sided pan over medium-high heat. Oil should be hot, 390° on a candy or deep-fry thermometer.

Drop batter by teaspoons into hot oil and fry until golden, turning as needed to even the color. Remove with slotted spoon and drain on absorbent paper towels. Allow to cool. Sprinkle with confectioners' sugar.

Makes about 2 dozen.

Dallas baker extraordinaire Betty Ablon makes rugelach, pecan-filled cookies, that are absolutely wonderful. They are also a Hanukkah tradition for some.

Rugelach

8 ounces unsalted butter, slightly softened
8 ounces cream cheese, slightly softened
2 cups all-purpose flour
½ cup apricot jam, heated to melt, then cooled (divided use)
¼ cup sugar plus 2 teaspoons cinnamon (divided use)
8 ounces (1 cup) finely chopped pecans or pecans and raisins to make 1 cup (divided use)

In a medium mixing bowl, beat together butter and cream cheese until creamy and light. Beat in flour, ½ cup at a time, to make a soft dough. Shape dough into a ball in the bowl and place bowl in refrigerator. Cover and chill dough for several hours for easier handling.

Preheat oven to 350°.

Divide dough in half. Roll out half the dough on a lightly floured board into a 12-inch circle, ⅙ inch thick, similar to pie crust. Brush lightly with ¼ cup apricot jam. Combine sugar and cinnamon. Sprinkle 1 tablespoon cinnamon sugar over jam. Spread with half the nuts. Cut circle into 16 wedges. Roll wedges, starting with the long side, and curve each pastry to form a crescent shape. Sprinkle crescents with 1 tablespoon cinnamon sugar.

Repeat using remaining dough and filling ingredients. Place on an ungreased cookie sheet and bake 18 to 20 minutes.

Makes 32 cookies.

Light sweets like macaroons and meringues are excellent for Hanukkah meals with meat on the menu. Both avoid dairy products.

Coconut Macaroons

Coconut Macaroons

4 large egg whites
¼ (scant) teaspoon salt
⅙ teaspoon cream of tartar
½ cup confectioners' sugar
1 teaspoon vanilla or almond extract
1 (8-ounce) package sweetened shredded coconut

Preheat oven to 350°. Line 2 baking sheets with parchment paper for baking.

Place egg whites in a medium bowl and allow to come to room temperature. Beat with an electric mixer on high speed until foamy. Add salt and cream of tartar. Continue beating. As whites begin to stiffen, slowly add sugar. Beat until very stiff and glossy.

Using a rubber spatula, gently fold in vanilla or almond flavoring and coconut. Drop by teaspoons on the parchment paper, about 1 inch apart. Batter should not spread.

Bake for 10 minutes. Remove baking sheet and rotate, back to front, in oven. Bake 5 to 10 minutes longer, until cookies are very light brown.

For a softer macaroon, slide parchment paper with macaroons onto a damp surface, such as a moist kitchen towel, and let them steam for 1 minute.

Using a spatula, transfer macaroons to racks to cool. Allow macaroons to dry several hours.

Makes 35 to 40 macaroons.

Macaroons are great cookies to make when you've had the oven hot for something else. Place meringues in an oven that has been turned off and cooled to about 200°. Leave in oven overnight.

Meringue Cookies

3 egg whites
¼ teaspoon salt
¼ teaspoon cream of tartar
½ cup granulated sugar
½ teaspoon vanilla
½ cup finely chopped pecans

Preheat oven to 200°. Line a cookie sheet with kitchen parchment paper.

In a large mixing bowl, beat egg whites with an electric mixer until frothy. Add salt and cream of tartar. Continue beating. As whites begin to stiffen, slowly add the sugar, a tablespoon at a time, until the mixture is stiff and glossy.

Using a rubber spatula, gently fold in vanilla and chopped pecans.

Drop batter by tablespoons onto the parchment paper about 1 inch apart. Bake for 1 hour or until meringues appear dry. Turn off oven and allow to cool in oven overnight.

Remove from cookie sheet and store in an airtight container. Makes 2 dozen.

⁓

Mini-strudels are another take on Hanukkah baking.

Mini-Strudels

4 ounces cream cheese, softened at room temperature
2 sticks (1 pound) butter, softened at room temperature
1 (8-ounce) carton sour cream
5–5½ cups all-purpose flour (sift before measuring)
1 (14-ounce) jar strawberry preserves
1 (14-ounce) jar apricot preserves
1 (6-ounce) package flaked coconut
2 cups raisins
1 (8-ounce) package chopped pecans
1 cup (approximately) granulated sugar (divided use)

In a large bowl, beat together cream cheese, butter, and sour cream. Gradually add flour, mixing by hand, to make a soft, but not sticky, dough. Shape dough into a ball and wrap tightly in plastic. Refrigerate overnight.

Preheat oven to 350°. Grease 2 cookie sheets.

Cut chilled dough into four pieces. Roll out each piece on a floured board into very thin rectangles. Spread strawberry preserves on 2 sections and apricot preserves on 2 sections. Sprinkle each section of dough with coconut, raisins, and pecans.

Fold over long sides to seal filling. Fold over ends to form long, narrow rectangles.

Place strudels, seam side down, on prepared cookie sheets. Sprinkle top of each strudel generously with granulated sugar. Cut through top layer of dough to make 1-inch pieces. Do not separate.

Bake for 45 minutes or until golden. Cool 15 minutes, then cut all the way through to make separate pieces. Separate and allow to cool.

Makes 64 (1-inch) pieces.

Standing Rib Roast of Beef,
p. 79; (clockwise) Twice-Baked
Potatoes, p. 87; Mince-Apple
Pie, p. 111, with Candied
Cranberries, p. 119; Minted
Carrots, p. 26; Texas Wine
Sauce, p. 83

Christmas

Nothing beats a Texas Christmas. No other holiday is more eagerly anticipated and so filled with memories.

A Texas Christmas reflects the richest blend of cultural influences of all the holidays, incorporating customs and traditions practiced by the many people who have come to call themselves Texans.

Twinkle lights in the pine trees of East Texas, luminaria in San Antonio, the capitol in Austin decked out for the holidays, elaborate theme decorations in department stores in Dallas and Houston, cowboy manger scenes in West Texas—all these are images of a Texas Christmas.

No traditions are more beautiful and symbolic than Hispanic folk expressions: luminaria (candlelit lanterns), *ristra* (dried red chili) wreaths, piñatas, and sparkling lights. Of course, German and English practices permeate Christmas celebrations as well, particularly in some of the signature foods: fruitcake, coconut cake, and eggnog.

While the scenes may differ with location, customs, and geography, many of the same holiday foods can be found in all locales throughout the state.

It is a holiday of mix-and-match traditions. Enchiladas and mince pie may show up on the same buffet.

Christmas Feasting

While the menu for Thanksgiving is virtually set in stone, Christmas feasts can be formal or casual. The main gathering may be on Christmas Eve as a nighttime meal. It may take place Christmas Day in the late morning as brunch, around the noon hour or early afternoon as dinner, or as an all-day open house.

And, often, families change their rituals from year to year, depending on a wide variety of circumstances, not the least of which is weather. As a native Texan, I can remember playing outdoors in shorts after opening presents on some Christmases, and, during other holiday seasons, waiting for frozen pipes to

---

TEX-MEX CHRISTMAS EVE MENU

Guacamole, 131

Pico de Gallo, 160

Chicken Mole, 60

with rice and warm flour tortillas

Refried Beans, 66

Sweet Tamales, 114

Mexican Hot Chocolate, 116

Flan, 117

CHRISTMAS BREAKFAST MENU

Fried Quail, 72

with Cream Gravy, 74

or Migas, 76

Cheddar Cheese Grits, 77

Texas Ambrosia (Fruit Salad), 31

or Fresh Spinach Salad with Texas Grapefruit, 89

Biscuits, 75

Kolaches (Czech Sweet Rolls), 78

Pumpkin Bread, 164

thaw so I could rinse the vegetables. Yes, Texas weather varies considerably during the winter. So do our tastes.

Christmas Eve

Christmas Eve is a time when many Texans hearken to their roots, varied though they may be. For some, it is a time to take special care to remember one's heritage through a particular dish or dishes. That might be sauerkraut and venison sausage, barbecue, or lasagna.

No Christmas Eve tradition is any richer than that of the Hispanic table. Mole is the dark, rich chocolate-and-ground-chile-based sauce so characteristic of Mexican holiday cuisine.

The following recipe is based on Dallas photographer Juan Garcia's mouthwatering description and adaptations of several recipes. Author Linda West Eckhardt (*The Only Texas Cookbook*) devised the shortcut addition of peanut butter to bottled mole sauce to better approximate the traditional sauce using dried, ground chilies, and toasted nuts and seeds.

In Mexico, this traditional dish uses turkey pieces.

Chicken Mole

8 pieces chicken (whole chicken cut up, or any
    combination of desired serving-size pieces such as legs,
    thighs, and breast halves) or 24 drummettes
1½ teaspoons salt, or to taste (divided use)
1 teaspoon pepper, or to taste
1 (8¼-ounce) jar mole sauce
½ cup enchilada sauce or tomato sauce
½–1 cup chicken stock
1 tablespoon smooth peanut butter
1 square dark, unsweetened chocolate
1 tablespoon sugar

Preheat oven to 350°. Heat a deep, ovenproof skillet or dutch oven over medium heat. Add chicken pieces and cook until

Chicken Mole, p. 60; Flan, p. 117;
A Real Margarita, p. 220;
Tamales, p. 63; Queso Salad,
p. 144; Salted Truffle Brownies
from Central Market baking mix

brown on all sides, about 20 minutes. Season chicken with 1 tea-spoon salt and pepper. Cover pan with lid and place in oven 20 to 30 minutes, until chicken juices run clear.

Meanwhile, in a large saucepan, combine mole sauce, enchilada or tomato sauce, and chicken stock, beginning with ½ cup. Add more as needed to adjust consistency and flavor. Heat to boiling; reduce heat to simmer. Stir in peanut butter, chocolate, and sugar. Cook and stir until chocolate is melted, about 5 minutes. Continue simmering 10 minutes longer. Season with ½ teaspoon salt, or to taste. If sauce seems too thick, add just enough water or chicken stock to thin to desired consistency.

Remove chicken from oven and pour sauce over chicken. Reduce oven to 300°. Return chicken to oven, covered, and bake for 30 to 40 minutes or until chicken is tender, almost falling off the bone.

Serve with white or Mexican rice (p. 65) or tortillas. This recipe doubles easily.

Makes 4 to 6 servings.

We always had tamales on Christmas and New Year's and sometimes mole, before or after Midnight Mass. I can taste that dark, red sauce right now and feel the chicken in my fingers, the meat so tender it slipped off the bones. It was served with rice, but you picked up the chicken with your fingers to eat it. The browner the sauce, the sweeter it was. The redder it was, the hotter.

—*Juan Garcia*

In many Hispanic households, no holiday is complete without a day or two of tamale making. This is a time for one generation to pass along family traditions to the next. It is a time for much merrymaking, laughter, some stories, perhaps a confession or two, and even a few tears.

Of course, there are Mexican restaurants and taquerias in most Texas cities where tamales can be purchased or special ordered. Many supermarkets even offer several varieties, both canned and frozen. But tamales, more than many other foods, are best seasoned by togetherness.

Allow two days (or one very long day) for tamale making. The filling improves when refrigerated overnight.

Tamale making is a three-stage process: cooking the filling, mixing the dough, and wrapping/steaming.

Traditional Pork Tamales

FILLING

- 3 pounds lean, boneless pork roast, or 2 pounds pork plus 1 pound boneless venison
- 8 cups water, or more as needed
- 2 cups chopped onion
- 4 cloves garlic, crushed
- 2 teaspoons salt, or to taste
- 2 teaspoons pepper, or to taste
- 1 (14.5-ounce) can enchilada sauce or 1 (15-ounce) can tomato sauce plus 1 tablespoon chili powder
- 1–2 teaspoons sugar, or to taste, optional

Cut pork (and venison) into 2- to 3-inch chunks and place in a large, heavy saucepan, dutch oven, or stockpot. Add enough water to just cover meat. Bring liquid to a boil over high heat. Reduce heat to simmer. Skim any foam that accumulates.

Add onion, garlic, salt, and pepper. Cover pot and cook over low heat for 2 to 3 hours, until meat is very tender and falling apart, adding more water if necessary to maintain level. Strain cooking liquid and reserve.

Cool meat enough to handle. Finely shred meat with fingers or use two forks to pull it into thin strips, going with the grain of the meat. Chopping does not produce the proper consistency.

Place meat in mixing bowl and add enchilada sauce or tomato sauce and chili powder. Add enough reserved stock (about 1 cup) to coat the meat with sauce. Mixture should not be watery; adjust liquid as necessary. Mix well and adjust seasoning with salt, pepper, and sugar. Cover and refrigerate overnight or chill several hours. Reserve and refrigerate any remaining broth for use in the dough.

DOUGH

- 10 cups masa harina (found alongside flour and cornmeal in the supermarket)
- 3–4 teaspoons salt, or to taste
- 2 teaspoons baking powder
- 2 cups lard (no substitutes)
- 3 cups reserved pork stock, heated (use chicken stock if more liquid is needed)

Combine masa harina, salt, and baking powder; set aside. Place lard in a large mixing bowl and beat at high speed with an electric beater until light and fluffy, about 3 to 5 minutes. Add masa mixture in 3 to 4 batches, alternately with the warm (not hot) broth, beating constantly.

Dough should be soft, but pliable, not watery. To test it, place a small piece of dough in a cup of water. If it floats, it is the right consistency.

WRAPPING AND STEAMING

60 dried corn husks
hot water

Several hours before preparing dough, rinse husks and remove any silk. Soak in hot water for several hours to soften.

TO SHAPE AND WRAP TAMALES

Pat dry the corn husks. Ready the dough and filling in assembly-line fashion. Wet your hands. Place a husk in the palm of one hand, and using the back of a spoon, spread about 2 tablespoons of the dough into a rectangle, starting at the wide end of the shuck. Leave about 1½ inches at the wide end of the shuck, about 3 inches at the pointed end. Spread dough to within ¾ inch of the sides. Spread 1 to 2 tablespoons tamale filling lengthwise down the center of the dough. Roll sides of tamales to seal the filling. Fold over wide end to seal bottom. Place folded side down on cookie sheet or large sheet of foil. Repeat until dough and filling are used. You should have about 4 dozen.

TO STEAM

Use a large tamale steamer or large pot with a rack or colander in the bottom. Fill bottom with water to depth of about 1 inch. Water should not touch the rack. Line rack with some of the remaining shucks. Arrange tamales vertically—wide, folded end down—on rack. Tamales should be packed, but not crammed, so that they will remain vertical. Cover the tamales with more corn husks or a layer of clean dish towels to prevent the tamales from absorbing too much water. They should be steamed, not immersed. Place lid on pot.

Bring water to a boil, reduce heat, and simmer for 1½ hours. Make sure water does not cook away during this time; add more as needed. Check tamales for doneness. Tamales are done when the masa easily separates from the husk and the tamale retains its shape. If not done, continue steaming for up to 3 hours or as needed.

If necessary, cook tamales in batches, reserving tamales in refrigerator until ready to steam.

Cooked tamales may be refrigerated several days or frozen for several weeks. Reheat, tightly wrapped in foil, in a 300° oven, about 30 minutes.

Makes about 4 dozen.

The red-orange rice you get in Mexican restaurants can be a meal in itself with refried beans and tortillas.

Mexican Rice

1 (16-ounce) can whole tomatoes, including liquid
1 tablespoon vegetable oil or bacon drippings
1 cup long-grain rice
1 cup chopped onion
½ cup finely chopped carrots
2 cloves garlic, finely chopped
1 (4-ounce) can chopped green chilies, drained,
    or 3 tablespoons finely chopped green bell pepper
1 (14½-ounce) can chicken or beef stock
¼ teaspoon cumin powder
1 teaspoon salt, or to taste
½ teaspoon pepper, or to taste

Empty tomatoes and their liquid into a 1-pint measuring cup. Use the back of a wooden spoon or edge of a knife to break tomatoes into bite-size pieces. Set aside.

Heat oil in a large skillet over medium heat. Add rice, stirring frequently, and cook until rice begins to brown. Add onion and carrots and cook until onions begin to soften. Lower heat, if necessary, to prevent rice from getting too dark. Stir in garlic.

Add tomatoes and their liquid, green chilies (or peppers), chicken or beef stock, cumin, salt, and pepper. Bring liquid to a boil. Reduce heat, cover, and simmer until rice is tender and liquid is absorbed, about 20 to 25 minutes. This recipe doubles easily.

Makes 4 servings.

Refried Beans

Soft and silky refried beans are the goo factor on many Mexican plates, the creamy foil for spicy sauces and toothy rice. Add enough liquid and oil to make them a silky mass, not too stiff, not too runny. And the way you like 'em. Here's how.

> 4 cups cooked pinto beans (see recipe below) or drained
>   pinto beans from 2 (16-ounce) cans
> 1 cup finely chopped onion
> 2 tablespoons lard, bacon drippings, or vegetable oil
> bean cooking liquid, stock, or water as needed
> salt and pepper to taste

Puree beans in food processor or blender with just enough liquid to achieve desired consistency. Or mash by hand using a potato masher. Place a medium skillet over medium-high heat. When skillet is hot, add onion and lard, bacon drippings, or oil. Lower heat and cook until onions are soft and lightly browned at the edges.

Add beans, stirring to mix well. Lower heat and cook until bubbly. Adjust texture as desired with bean cooking liquid, stock, or water. Season to taste with salt and pepper.

Makes 8 servings.

For additional flavor, use stock in the cooking liquid. It can be chicken, beef, or vegetable stock along with water. Or just use water.

Texas Pinto Beans

1 pound dry pinto beans
3 to 4 strips bacon, cut into 1-inch pieces
2 cups chopped onion
4 cloves garlic, crushed
1 fresh jalapeño
chicken, beef, or vegetable stock; water; or a combination
   of liquid as needed
salt to taste

Rinse beans in colander. Place in a large pot with enough water to cover. Soak overnight or place over high heat and bring to a boil. Cook for 1 minute. Turn off heat, cover pot, and soak beans for 1 hour.

After beans have soaked, pour off soaking liquid through colander. Rinse beans a couple of times. Rinse pot and place over medium heat, with bacon, onion, and garlic. Cook until bacon gives up its fat and onions are translucent and beginning to soften.

Return beans to pot and cover with enough liquid to cover by 1 inch. Add jalapeño. Bring liquid to a boil over high heat. Lower temperature; cover and simmer for 2 to 3 hours or until beans are tender. When beans are tender, add salt to taste.

To achieve a creamy "sauce" for the beans, remove 1 cup of beans and liquid from the pot and process in a food processor or blender or simply mash with the back of a spoon or a ricer. Return to pot.

Makes 10 to 12 servings.

Oyster stew is a holiday tradition in many Southern homes as well as homes that observe the Catholic tradition of abstaining from meat on Christmas Eve. As if this oyster stew represented a sacrifice!

My friend Martha Hershey, now a longtime Dallas resident, recalls a creamy, steaming hot bowl of oyster stew as part of her family's New Orleans Christmas Eve menu.

This is a classic version using small oysters, about 24 to the pint.

Gulf Coast Oyster Stew

1 cup chopped onion
3 tablespoons butter
1 quart half-and-half
1 cup whole milk
½ teaspoon salt
½ teaspoon cayenne pepper or to taste
1 pint fresh raw oysters, undrained (about 2 dozen)
1 bunch green onions, sliced

Place onion and butter in large saucepan over medium heat. Cook onion until soft and transparent, about 5 minutes. Stir in half-and-half, milk, salt, and cayenne to taste. Simmer over low heat about 5 minutes to allow flavors to meld.

Recipe may be prepared ahead to this point and refrigerated until ready to reheat and serve.

Add oysters and their liquor to hot cream mixture. Cook just until edges of oysters curl; do not allow mixture to boil. Remove from heat. Serve immediately. Garnish individual servings with a sprinkling of green onions.

Makes 6 to 8 servings.

Janis and Joe Pinnelli make a mean pan of lasagna at their Austin home on Christmas Eve. Joe, the true Texas *paisano*, makes the sauce. Janis puts the whole thing together.

Joe developed the sauce recipe by watching his grandmother cooking in Italy and by trial and error in his own kitchen. Use it any time a basic marinara sauce is called for.

Christmas Eve Lasagna

THE SAUCE

4 (28-ounce) cans whole tomatoes
1 (6-ounce) can tomato paste
2 tablespoons dried crushed oregano (not powdered)
1 tablespoon dried thyme
1 tablespoon dried rosemary
1 teaspoon salt, or to taste

4 garlic cloves, crushed
¼ cup virgin olive oil
2 tablespoons sugar

THE FILLING

3 cups fresh ricotta cheese
2 eggs, lightly beaten
2 tablespoons parsley flakes
½ cup grated Romano cheese
1 teaspoon salt, or to taste
½ teaspoon pepper, or to taste
1 pound lasagna noodles, cooked according to package
   directions
1 (16-ounce) pound mozzarella cheese, sliced
grated Parmesan cheese, for passing at table

TO MAKE SAUCE

Since sauce scorches easily, use a large, heavy-bottomed saucepan, stockpot, or dutch oven, preferably with a nonstick surface.

Place canned tomatoes and their liquid into the pan. Use a small paring knife to remove any tomato cores. Add tomato paste.

Use hands (or back of a large wooden spoon) to crush the tomatoes and combine with the tomato paste. Tomatoes should be in small pieces. The mixture should be soupy and lumpy.

Combine oregano, thyme, rosemary, and salt into a blender. Blend to a smooth powder.

Add powdered spices, garlic, and olive oil to tomatoes, stirring well. Place pot on stove over low heat. Bring liquid to a simmer and simmer for 1 hour and 30 minutes. Stir almost continually during cooking since sauce scorches easily. Use a spatula to scrape sauce from bottom to avoid sticking.

Add sugar 15 minutes before the end of cooking. Do not add sugar too soon, or sauce will stick. Overcooking will result in a bitter taste. For optimum flavor, make the sauce a day ahead and refrigerate overnight.

Use over spaghetti or any other recipe that calls for a rich marinara sauce. The sauce freezes well. Reheat and simmer to desired consistency.

TO ASSEMBLE LASAGNA

Allow sauce to cool. Meanwhile, stir together in a large bowl the ricotta cheese, eggs, parsley, Romano cheese, salt, and pepper.

Preheat oven to 350°. Line bottom of large, flat baking dish or roasting pan (at least 9 × 13 inches) with half the cooked noodles. Cover with half the cheese mixture, half the sliced mozzarella, and a generous layer of sauce, thick enough to seal the edges. Repeat with remaining noodles, cheese mixture, and sliced mozzarella. Cover with a generous layer of sauce. Reserve and heat some sauce for passing at table.

Bake lasagna, uncovered, for 30 to 45 minutes or until heated through. Cut into squares and serve. Serve with additional sauce and Parmesan cheese, passed at the table.

VARIATION

* Double ingredients for filling and make 2 pans of lasagna. Add 1 pound of crumbled, cooked, and drained Italian sausage or ground beef to sauce along with spices. Cook as above.

Makes 8 to 10 servings.

This recipe first hit our table on Christmas Day but in recent years it's become a Christmas Eve buffet favorite. This decadent dish tastes deceptively light, but no concoction with this much cream, cheese, butter, and silky seafood is truly "light." Still, it doesn't weigh heavy on the palate compared to the next day's feast, often featuring roast beef, crown roast of pork, or a turducken. "Heavenly" is the operative word for this dreamy pasta dish.

White Lasagna with Seafood

12 no-boil lasagna noodles
4 tablespoons butter
1 small onion, finely chopped
3 cloves garlic, minced
4 tablespoons flour
2 cups half-and-half
1 cup whole milk
1 cup grated Romano cheese
½ teaspoon salt or to taste
¼ teaspoon pepper or to taste
¾ pound medium shrimp, peeled
¾ pound sea scallops, cut in half or smaller pieces if very large
½ cup grated Parmesan cheese

Preheat oven to 375 F. Spray a 9 × 13-inch baking pan with vegetable oil cooking spray. Set aside.

Melt the butter in a large saucepan and cook the onion over low heat until translucent and very soft, about 5 to 7 minutes. Add the garlic and cook a minute or two longer.

Stir the flour into the onions with a whisk and cook for 1 or 2 minutes. Gradually, add the half-and-half, then the milk, stirring constantly. Raise heat to medium until sauce begins to thicken and bubble. Add the Romano cheese and stir until very smooth. Add salt and pepper. Remove from heat; using a ladle or large spoon, reserve about 1 cup sauce; set aside.

Return remaining sauce to low heat, fold in shrimp and scallops; cook just until the shrimp turn pink. Remove from heat.

To assemble lasagna, spoon about 2 tablespoons reserved sauce (without seafood) into the prepared baking dish, spreading to coat the bottom of the dish evenly. Place 4 noodles lengthwise into the pan, side-by-side. Spoon half the seafood over the noodles, distributing shrimp and scallops evenly. Layer on 4 more noodles and the remaining seafood, reserving as much sauce as possible.

For the top layer, add 4 more noodles and cover with any remaining sauce. All the seafood should be between the first two layers of lasagna noodles. The top (third) layer should be sauce only. Make sure noodles are coated with sauce. Use the reserved 1 cup sauce to make sure the top, edges and ends are well-coated. Top with Parmesan cheese. Cover with aluminum foil and bake for 20 minutes. Remove foil and bake an additional 5 to 10 minutes or until Parmesan is golden.

Makes 8 servings.

Fail-Safe Precaution: Just in case you need more sauce, make sure you have a container of ready-made Alfredo sauce as an emergency stash. It's a quick and easy way to fill in the sauce if you think the lasagna needs more liquid before it goes into the oven.

Christmas Breakfast

Christmas breakfast can be as simple as bakery pastries or as elaborate as fried quail with cheese grits and Texas ambrosia. It is a wonderful meal at which to blend the best of several traditions, country gravy with sausage and fluffy biscuits, Tex-Mex eggs, Southern-fried quail, and various pastries including Czech kolaches.

Whether you buy them or bag them, quail are a wonderful delicacy. The tender birds are flavorful and adapt well to many methods of cooking. Pen-raised quail, available in supermarkets and by mail order, are larger than the wild birds. If you're lucky enough to have wild quail, make a few extra.

Fried Quail

8 quail
1 cup buttermilk
1 cup unbleached flour
2 teaspoons salt, or to taste
1 teaspoon pepper, or to taste
oil for frying

Rinse quail and pat dry. Split backs of quail so birds can open flat, breast up with legs and wings flattened.

Place quail in resealable plastic bag. Pour buttermilk over and allow to marinate 30 minutes to several hours, or overnight. Remove quail from buttermilk and allow to drain.

Combine flour, salt, and pepper in large plastic bag, shaking to mix well. Drop quail into flour mixture, one at a time, shaking well to coat evenly. Remove from bag and place on a layer of wax paper. Repeat with remaining quail. Allow quail to sit for 10 to 20 minutes to "set" the batter.

Fried Quail, p. 72, with Cream Gravy, p. 74, Cheddar Cheese Grits, p. 77, and sliced tomatoes

Heat 1 inch vegetable or corn oil in a heavy skillet, prefer-ably cast iron. Oil should be hot, about 375°.

Gently, slide a quail into hot oil, breast side down. Allow oil to recover temperature so that the quail floats before adding next bird. Fry 2 to 3 birds at a time. Each quail should have room to float in the pan without touching. Cook until golden and crisp on breast side, about 5 minutes. Turn and fry on back side until golden brown and crisp, about 3 to 4 minutes.

Because quail is white meat, it cooks rather quickly, like chicken breast. Remove quail from skillet and drain briefly on paper towels. Keep warm. Serve with Cream Gravy or Texas Wine Sauce (p. 83).

Makes 8 servings.

Serve with Cream Gravy or Texas Wine Sauce (p. 83).

Smothered Quail

Preheat oven to 325°. Arrange fried quail in a 9 × 13-inch baking dish. Pour in about ⅛ inch water, Cream Gravy, or Texas Wine Sauce. Cover with foil and bake for 30 to 45 min-utes. Serve with additional gravy or sauce.

This is the mother's milk of Texas cooking. It can be found on plates from breakfast through dinner.

Cream Gravy

3 tablespoons vegetable oil, melted butter, or drippings from frying
¼ cup flour
1 cup (each) warm milk and warm water or stock, more liquid if needed
1 teaspoon salt, or to taste
1 teaspoon pepper, or to taste

Heat oil, butter, or drippings in large skillet over medium heat. (If making gravy after cooking sausage or frying quail or other meat, pour off all but three tablespoons of drip-pings. Keep the browned bits in the bottom of the skillet.)

Because of health and time concerns, frying—once everyman's (and woman's)—cooking method has become something of a lost art. There's no better time than the holidays to cultivate this vanishing technique. My mother, Dorothy Griffith, the aforementioned queen of gravy, also ranked as the high priestess of frying. She recommended this test to see if the oil is hot enough: pinch off a 1-inch piece of white bread. Drop it in the oil. Bread will pop to the surface and immediately begin browning at the edges when oil is the right temperature for frying.

Stir in flour and cook until bubbly, scraping up any bits that may stick to bottom of pan. Add milk and water or stock, stirring constantly with wire whisk or the back of a slotted spoon. Lower heat and simmer until thickened. Add salt and pepper to taste. Serve over Fried Quail, mashed potatoes, or just about any meat or fowl, particularly if it is fried.

Sausage Gravy

Crumble ¼ to ½ pound bulk sausage into skillet over medium heat. Cook until brown. Drain sausage on paper toweling. Reserve 3 tablespoons of pan drippings. Discard remainder. Make gravy as above, using pan drippings. Add cooked sausage when gravy thickens. Season to taste. Serve over biscuits or scrambled eggs.

Makes 8 servings.

This is a basic biscuit recipe. Knead the dough as little as possible. But making the extra "turn" or fold on the dough gives lighter, fluffier biscuits. The principle is the same as puff pastry.

Use self-rising or all-purpose flour for biscuits. But know this: Self-rising flour with built-in leavening is a Southern staple. Using all-purpose flour for biscuits requires the addition of baking powder so the biscuits will rise.

Biscuits

2 cups sifted all-purpose or self-rising flour
3 teaspoons baking powder, omit if using self-rising flour
1 teaspoon salt
⅓ cup shortening
¾ cup cold milk

Preheat oven to 450°.
Combine self-rising flour and salt or all-purpose flour, baking powder, and salt in work bowl of food processor. Pulse several times to combine and aerate. Or sift together flour, baking powder if using, and salt.

Add shortening to work bowl and pulse to combine. Or cut in shortening using two knives, a pastry cutter, or fingers. Mixture should resemble coarse cornmeal. With motor running, add milk and process just until soft dough forms. Or make a well in dry ingredients, stir in milk, and mix just until soft dough forms.

Turn dough out onto lightly floured board. Knead lightly 2 or 3 times and pat with fingers or roll out dough about ½ inch thick. Fold over dough in thirds and reroll into a ½-inch-thick oblong, handling as little as possible.

Cut with a 2-inch biscuit cutter or flour the rim of a water glass and use as a cutter. Place biscuits on ungreased baking sheet and bake 10 to 12 minutes until golden brown.

Makes 10 to 12 biscuits.

This is a traditional Tex-Mex recipe for scrambled eggs.

Migas

6 eggs
6 tablespoons water
½ teaspoon salt, or to taste
¼ teaspoon pepper, or to taste
3 corn tortillas
1 tablespoon vegetable oil
½ cup onion, chopped fine
½ cup chopped fresh mild chile, such as green, poblano or Anaheim (California) pepper (seeded)
1 cup chopped tomato, optional
½ cup grated cheddar cheese

Combine eggs and water, 2 tablespoons at a time, beating until frothy. Add salt and pepper to taste. Set aside.

Cut tortillas into bite-size pieces, about the size of small corn chips. Heat oil in large skillet over medium heat. Add tortilla pieces, stirring to distribute evenly and cook until crisp, 2 to 3 minutes. Drain on paper toweling and reserve.

Add onion to skillet and cook until soft and golden around the edges. Add green chilies and cook until softened, 2 to 3 minutes. Pour eggs into skillet. Add tortilla chips. Stir to evenly cook eggs.

When eggs are almost firm, add tomatoes and cheese; stir. Cook just until cheese melts and eggs are set. Serve immediately.

Makes 6 to 8 servings.

Cheddar Cheese Grits

4 cups milk
4 tablespoons butter (divided use)
1 cup grits, quick-cooking or old-fashioned (not instant)
1 cup shredded cheddar cheese
1 teaspoon salt, or to taste
½ teaspoon pepper, or to taste
2–3 drops red pepper sauce, or to taste

Combine milk, 2 tablespoons butter, and grits over medium heat in a large saucepan. When milk begins to boil, lower heat. Simmer and stir over low heat, according to package directions, about 3 to 5 minutes for quick-cooking grits, 10 to 12 minutes for old-fashioned, or until thickened.

Remove from heat. Stir in 2 tablespoons butter, cheese, salt, pepper, and red pepper sauce, to taste. Adjust texture with additional milk, if needed. May be made ahead, stored in refrigerator, and reheated in oven or on top of stove over low heat.

Makes 8 servings.

There are two Texas "tweener" towns known for their kolache bakeries: the town of West, just north of Waco on I-35 about halfway between Dallas and Austin, and Ellinger, also about halfway between Houston and Austin on State Highway 71. Can't make it to West or Ellinger? Try these.

Kolaches (Czech Sweet Rolls)

2 packages dry yeast
½ cup lukewarm (105°–115°) water
1½ cups warm milk
½ cup butter
½ cup sugar
1 teaspoon salt
1 egg, beaten
5–6 cups flour
fillings (see below)

Sprinkle yeast over warm water, stirring to activate. Set aside. Heat milk to almost boiling. Remove from heat. Add butter and stir to melt. Add sugar and salt. Pour into large mixing bowl and allow to cool to lukewarm. Stir in egg and add yeast mixture.

Add flour gradually, about 2 cups at a time, stirring after each addition to make a soft, sticky dough. Do not add too much flour or kolaches will be dense and dry. Cover and let rise until doubled in size, about 1 hour. Begin preparing fillings while dough rises.

Grease a baking sheet well. Rub hands with grease, too. Using well-greased hands, shape dough into 2-inch balls. Place on prepared baking sheet about 2 inches apart. Cover with damp cloth and let rise again until doubled in size, about 30 to 45 minutes.

Preheat oven to 350°. Using your thumb, make an indention in the center of each roll, leaving a 1-inch rim. Allow to rest 10 minutes. Fill with about 1 tablespoon fruit or cheese filling and bake for 20 to 25 minutes or until golden.

Makes about 3 dozen.

FILLINGS

* Combine 1 cup dried fruit (6-ounce package of apricots, prunes, or apples) in just enough water to cover in a small saucepan. Bring water to a boil, reduce heat, and simmer until fruit is soft, about 10 to 12 minutes. Drain fruit and chop fine. Return to saucepan along

with 1 cup sugar, 1½ teaspoons lemon juice, and 4 tablespoons butter. Cook and stir over low heat until mixture thickens like jam, about 10 minutes. Cool completely.

* Combine 1 cup cream cheese or dry-curd cottage cheese with ½ cup sugar, 1 egg yolk, 1 teaspoon vanilla, ⅛ teaspoon salt, and 3 tablespoons melted butter. Mix until smooth.

Christmas Dinner

The big sit-down isn't reserved for Thanksgiving alone. But there's much more latitude with the Christmas menu. Often, a Christmas table will hold a variety of meats: perhaps ham and turkey, maybe venison or a beef roast.

Christmas is a time when the focus is scattered: religious celebrations, gifts, decorations, parties. Food is important, but just a part of the mix. That gives a Texas cook lots of room for family favorites.

And it doesn't matter when you sit down to a Christmas dinner. It can be on Christmas day, Christmas Eve, or anytime during the holiday when family and friends can be together.

Beef is as almost as traditional for Christmas as turkey is for Thanksgiving. In a state where much of the lore and culture is based on ranching, that is understandable. But the hunting tradition is important here also. So you'll find plenty of wild game recipes on holiday tables.

As with Thanksgiving, getting a head start on Christmas dinner is the key to success in timing. This is even more difficult to achieve at Christmas because there is so much more going on. The good news? The meal can be simpler, at least in terms of the number of dishes required to fulfill expectations of tradition.

Standing Rib Roast of Beef

1 (5–8-pound) standing beef rib roast
3–4 cloves garlic, cut into slivers, optional
2 teaspoons salt, or to taste
1 teaspoon pepper, or to taste

Remove roast from refrigerator 1 hour before roasting to allow meat to come to room temperature. Preheat oven to 325°.

If desired, pierce surface of roast at intervals with the tip of a sharp knife or ice pick and insert a sliver of garlic.

Place roast, fat side up, in open roasting pan. Place it on a rack, or let the ribs serve as a natural rack to keep the meat from sitting in the fat as it drips into the pan.

Do not add liquid to the pan; do not cover. Place meat in oven and roast for 14 to 18 minutes per pound, or until meat thermometer reads 140° for rare and up to 170° for well done.

Medium rare, about 145°, is optimum for flavor and tenderness. A roast that registers 140° to 145° when the meat thermometer is inserted in the thickest part, not touching fat or bone, will ensure that there are nice rare slices in the middle. Naturally, slices from the exterior will tend to be more done, thus ensuring a degree of doneness to make everyone happy.

Slice ½ inch thick.

Makes 10 to 12 servings.

VARIATION

* For Beef Tenderloin, ask butcher to fold over and tie ends of 5-pound beef tenderloin to create a roast of uniform thickness. (Plan on 3 servings per pound for this boneless cut.) Insert slivers of fresh garlic, if desired. Rub lightly with butter or vegetable oil. Preheat oven to 400°. Place on a rack in a shallow roasting pan. Follow instructions for 500° Method.

THE 500° METHOD FOR PERFECT ROAST BEEF

For a couple of years, I hosted a weekday call-in radio talk show about food on KRLD in Dallas. This was the most-requested recipe ever. Probably because it is failsafe. This works for beef roasts such as standing rib or tenderloins that are best served medium rare. It is not a satisfactory method for preparing pot roasts or other less tender cuts that benefit from long, slow cooking to make fork tender.

Here's how it works: Remove any size beef roast from refrigerator 1 hour before roasting. Preheat oven to 500°. Season roast as desired. Place roast in open roasting pan with shallow sides and cook for exactly 5 minutes per pound. At that point, turn off oven. DO NOT open the oven door. Leave

Tip: Allow 2 to 3 servings per pound when buying a standing rib roast. Ask the butcher to separate the roast from the bones, and then to tie it back in position. This allows for easier slicing while retaining the natural roasting rack formed by the ribs. Remove string before slicing.

roast (no matter what size) in oven with heat turned off for exactly 2 hours. Remove roast from oven. It will be cooked medium rare.

Example: an 8-pound roast should cook for 40 minutes at 500°. Immediately, turn off oven. Do not open the oven door. Leave roast in oven for 2 hours.

Caution: this method produces a lot of spatter in the oven if you're cooking a roast such as a standing rib with a thick layer of fat. Don't be surprised at some smoke, and expect to clean the oven.

Spiral-cut hams with a honey crust have put a serious dent in the home preparation of ham and undoubtedly increased consumption because they're so darn good . . . and convenient. But for a classic, home-baked ham, try this recipe.

Brown Sugar–Baked Ham

1 (8–10-pound) fully cooked ham, bone-in
2–3 tablespoons ground cinnamon
2 tablespoons ground cloves
1 tablespoon yellow or dijon mustard
whole cloves, optional
½ cup brown sugar, packed
1 tablespoon flour

Preheat oven to 300°–325°. If using a cured ham with skin on, cut away skin from ham, but leave the fat. Rub ham with cinnamon and ground cloves to cover completely. Wrap tightly in foil and bake for 15 minutes per pound. Cool ham slightly and scrape away cinnamon and cloves; discard.

Coat ham with thin smear of mustard. If desired, cut diamond pattern into fat layer and place a whole clove in each diamond as a garnish. Combine brown sugar with flour. Pat brown sugar mixture over ham to evenly cover fat layer. Use additional brown sugar, if needed, to thoroughly coat ham. Return ham, uncovered, to oven for 30 to 35 minutes to melt and caramelize the sugar. Cool before slicing and serving.

Makes 10 to 12 servings.

The choicest cut of venison is the backstrap, which resembles a beef tenderloin in appearance (although smaller) and tenderness. Treat as you would beef; roast it or grill it no more than medium rare, although rare with a warm center is preferable because the cut is so naturally lean.

Roast Venison Backstrap

2 (1½–2-pound) venison backstraps
1 tablespoon vegetable oil
1–2 teaspoons each salt and pepper, or to taste; or substitute 1 to 2 teaspoons favorite steak seasoning blend, to taste
2 tablespoons butter

If backstraps are more than 2 inches thick, preheat oven to 400°.

Rub backstraps with oil and season to taste with salt and pepper or steak seasoning blend.

Heat a heavy skillet with ovenproof handle over medium-high heat. Lightly coat with nonstick cooking spray. Add backstraps and cook on all sides until brown. Internal temperature should not cook past medium rare (140° on a meat thermometer). Thick backstraps may require 3 to 5 minutes in the oven to cook to desired degree of doneness.

Remove from heat and allow juices to settle, about 10 minutes. Wrap backstrap in foil to keep warm.

Over medium heat, whisk butter into pan juices, 1 tablespoon at a time, just until melted. Adjust seasoning as desired.

Place backstrap on serving platter and slice into ½- to 1-inch-thick medallions. Drizzle with pan juices.

If desired, serve with Texas Wine Sauce (p. 83) or other favorite sauce.

Makes 6 to 8 servings.

VARIATION

* To grill backstraps, light coals and cook until gray ash covers the surface. Oil and season backstrap as above.

Tip: For some reason, many cooks are afraid to stop cooking when wild game reaches the rare or medium-rare stage. No wonder they often find the taste to be gamy. Because wild game is so lean, it is juicier and has a more subtle flavor when it isn't roasted or grilled to well done temperature. Legendary wild-game cook and restaurateur Matt Martinez observed that wild game is less suspect than many of the commercial meats we eat because the wild game diet is all-natural. It hasn't been injected with growth hormones or antibiotics. So don't make the mistake of overcooking wild game in the name of food safety. With tender cuts like whole backstrap or backstrap medallions, go for the same degree of doneness as you would prime beef.

Place on hot grill and cook as you would a steak, until medium rare, turning once to cook all sides. Remove from grill and spread butter over top of each backstrap. Slice and serve with accumulated juices.

Makes 6 to 8 servings.

———

This particular sauce will work well for beef or wild game, including game birds, but it is particularly nice with roast prime rib of beef or roast venison backstrap.

Texas Wine Sauce

- 2 cups beef stock
- 1 cup dry red wine (preferably from Texas)
- 2 tablespoons butter
- 1½ tablespoons cornstarch
- 2 tablespoons water
- 1 teaspoon each salt and pepper, or to taste, or substitute your favorite seasoning blend

In a medium saucepan, combine stock and wine. Place over high heat and bring liquid to a boil. Reduce heat and cook until liquid is reduced by half to make about 1½ cups sauce.

Whisk in butter. Combine cornstarch and water to make a smooth paste. Whisk into sauce and cook over low heat, just until thickened. Add salt and pepper or seasoning blend to taste. Keep warm in a thermos bottle or double boiler until ready to serve. Reheat gently; do not allow to boil.

Makes 1½ cups, about 6 servings.

———

This is a luxurious add-on. Horseradish cream is traditional with roast beef. Throw in some lump crab, as I did one Christmas, and the effect is particularly festive. This makes a beautiful medium-rare beef tenderloin or standing rib roast even more spectacular.

Tip: Add pan juices from cooking to sauce for additional flavor and richness. If pan juices are defatted, add all the juices to the sauce and thicken to desired consistency. If adding pan drippings (mostly fat), add 2 tablespoons and omit butter.

Horseradish Cream
with Lump Crabmeat

½ cup heavy cream, chilled
½ cup sour cream, chilled
½ teaspoon salt, or to taste
4 tablespoons bottled horseradish, drained
8 ounces lump crabmeat, drained

Place heavy cream in small bowl and beat with electric beaters until soft peaks form. Fold in sour cream, salt, and horseradish. Refrigerate until ready to serve.

Just before serving, fold in crabmeat. Serve with roast beef, grilled steaks, or seafood for dolloping.

Makes 2 cups.

Like most families, our children, now grown, insist on certain dishes each holiday because "we always" have, say, Gram's dressing for Thanksgiving, beef at Christmas, and a "shore dinner" around the Fourth of July. One food tradition got added late in our family's life, just as the youngest was heading off to college: tortilla soup as the starter course for Christmas dinner. It was 1998 and the year this cookbook was first published. Perusing it, one of us (we can't remember who) came upon Dotty's tortilla soup recipe (p. 142) and it was immediately added to the traditions. Now, instead of Dad making it, our older daughter, Kelly, has the responsibility. And the newest member of our family, five-year-old Ella, already loves it and expects it. This past Christmas, as we were leaving to spend the holiday with all of them, Dotty brought us all the fixins for tortilla soup: the soup, the avocados, the tortilla chips, even the sour cream. When we unpacked it, Kelly was momentarily wounded. "I was going to make it," she said. "You didn't have to do it." Her disappointment melted when she learned it was the same tortilla soup, only made by the original!

—Michael and Terri Burke

Some holidays just aren't complete without a retro congealed salad to add color and a touch of sweet. Here is a sixties classic that also goes well with roasted or grilled meats.

Cherry Cola Salad

1 (16 ½-ounce) can dark cherries
1 (8-ounce) can crushed pineapple
2 packages black cherry gelatin
1 (12-ounce) can cola (not diet)
1 cup chopped pecans
lettuce leaves and mayonnaise for garnish, optional

Lightly coat a 1½-quart gelatin mold or 9 × 9-inch casserole with nonstick cooking spray. Set aside.

Drain juice from cherries and pineapple; reserve juice in 2-cup measure. Add just enough water to make 2 cups. Heat juice and water to boiling. Combine with gelatin in a medium mixing bowl. Stir until gelatin dissolves, about 2 to 3 minutes. Pour cola into gelatin.

Place gelatin mixture in refrigerator and chill until gelatin begins to set. The mixture should be thick and somewhat jiggly, but not firm. Fold in drained pineapple and cherries and pecans. Mixture should be thick enough to suspend ingredients evenly throughout gelatin.

Transfer to prepared mold or dish. Refrigerate until firm.

Unmold by dipping bottom of mold into hot water and inverting onto a serving dish. Loosen sides with edge of knife, if needed, or cut gelatin into 3-inch squares and serve on lettuce leaves. Garnish each square with a small dollop of mayonnaise, if desired.

Makes 10 to 12 servings.

A Christmas table may, or may not, include turkey and dressing. But there's always room for some potatoes. Really Whomped-Up Mashed Potatoes with Sour Cream and Cheese (see p. 23) are a classic, but consider these classic scalloped potatoes as well.

Scalloped Potatoes

4 to 5 large (2 to 3 pounds) russet potatoes, peeled, and
  sliced very thin
1 teaspoon salt or to taste
½ teaspoon pepper or to taste
½ cup butter or as needed
2 cups (1 pint) half-and-half or as needed

Preheat oven to 350°. Rub a 9 × 13-inch baking dish with soft butter.

Place a single layer of potato slices in bottom of dish, with edges overlapping. Season with salt and pepper. Dot liberally with small pieces of butter. Pour over just enough half-and-half to lightly coat potatoes.

Repeat, layering potatoes, salt, pepper, butter, and half-and-half until all potatoes have been layered into dish. Top with additional half-and-half to moisten potatoes well. Cover with foil.

Place in oven and bake, covered, for 30 minutes. Remove foil and bake another 30 minutes or until potatoes are tender and edges are golden brown. Add additional cream as needed to prevent potatoes from becoming too dry.

Makes 8 to 10 servings.

Potatoes Au Gratin

5 large (about 2½ to 3 pounds) russet potatoes
1¼ cups shredded cheddar cheese
6 tablespoons butter (divided use)
1 cup sour cream
1 teaspoon salt, or to taste
½ teaspoon pepper, or to taste
3 green onions, chopped, including green parts, optional
½ cup crushed potato chips or cracker crumbs, optional

Preheat oven to 325°–350°. Coat a 2-quart casserole dish with nonstick spray.

Place whole, unpeeled potatoes in large saucepan with enough cold water to cover. Cook over high heat until water boils. Reduce heat so that water continues at a slow boil and cook potatoes until easily pierced with a fork, about 30 minutes.

Allow to cool slightly. Peel off skins and cut potatoes into quarters. Place in large mixing bowl. Using a potato masher or fork, coarsely mash potatoes so the texture is crumbly, almost a chopped consistency. Set aside.

Combine cheese and 4 tablespoons butter in large saucepan over low heat. Stir until cheese is almost melted. Remove from heat and stir in sour cream. Fold cheese mixture into potatoes along with salt, pepper, and onions.

Melt 2 tablespoons butter. Sprinkle crushed potato chips or cracker crumbs over top of potatoes, if desired. Drizzle melted butter over top of casserole.

Makes 10 to 12 servings.

We make these as a tribute to my children's grandmother, the legendary Janet Stephenson of Kansas City, Missouri. Gram, as three generations know her, is famous for her twice-baked potatoes, although on any given day she'd rather have a Coke and a Snickers bar.

Twice-Baked Potatoes

5 large (2½ to 3 pounds) russet potatoes, unpeeled
1 (3-ounce) package cream cheese, softened at room temperature
½ cup sour cream
¾–1¼ cups warm milk or half-and-half
6 tablespoons butter (divided use)
1 teaspoon salt, or to taste
½ teaspoon white pepper, or to taste
6 tablespoons grated Parmesan or cheddar cheese, optional

Preheat oven to 425°. Rinse potatoes and dry. Pierce each potato several times with a fork. Rub each potato lightly with butter. Place potatoes directly on middle rack of oven and bake until tender, about 1 hour to 1 hour and 15 minutes. The potatoes should yield when squeezed lightly wearing an oven mitt.

Remove potatoes from oven. Wearing an oven mitt or heatproof glove on one hand, hold potato and slice in half lengthwise. Scoop out hot potato pulp into a large mixing bowl; reserve potato shells. Be careful not to tear shells.

Using electric beaters, beat baked potato pulp on low speed, adding cream cheese, sour cream, milk, 4 tablespoons butter, salt, and pepper. When potatoes begin to get smooth, increase speed to high and continue beating until quite smooth. Adjust consistency and flavor with milk, cream cheese, butter, and sour cream, as needed. The texture should be smooth and spoonable, but not runny. Season to taste with salt and pepper.

Spoon potato mixture back into shells, creating small peaks. Sprinkle each potato with cheese. Potatoes may be refrigerated at this point and reheated later for serving.

Melt remaining 2 tablespoons butter and drizzle over potatoes. Bake in 325°–350° oven until potatoes are hot, cheese melts, and edges are golden, about 20 to 25 minutes.

Stuffed potato shells may be made ahead and refrigerated until just before serving time. Finish baking, allowing 30 to 35 minutes for reheating and browning.

Makes 10 to 12 servings.

The Rio Grande Valley is a garden of eatin' (excuse the pun, I just couldn't resist) with the variety of fruits and vegetables grown in this semitropical climate. Red grapefruit are the best known of the winter crops, but other vegetables, such as spinach, abound. There are, of course, some vegetable dishes that lend themselves to winter feasting regardless of season, such as green beans and corn.

Dress up Texas vegetables for the holiday according to Lone Star standards.

Fresh Spinach Salad
with Texas Grapefruit

SALAD

2 (10-ounce) packages fresh spinach, or 4 bunches leaf
spinach
2 Ruby Red or Rio Red grapefruit, peeled, or 1 (11-ounce)
can mandarin orange sections, drained
½ cup chopped, toasted pecans

SHERRY VINAIGRETTE

½ cup light olive oil
¼ cup sherry vinegar
½ teaspoon salt, or to taste
¼ teaspoon pepper, or to taste
½ teaspoon maple syrup
⅛ teaspoon minced serrano chile, optional

Tear spinach leaves from stems. Place spinach leaves in sink full of cold water. Place in colander to drain. Transfer to several layers of dish towels to dry completely. If using bunch spinach, rinse two or three times in sink full of water to remove any sand.

Dry spinach leaves between layers of dish towels. Place spinach leaves in large salad bowl, tearing large leaves into bite-size pieces. Separate grapefruit into sections and cut sections into bite-size pieces. Toss with spinach. Pour sherry vinaigrette over salad and toss to evenly coat ingredients. Garnish with chopped pecans.

Makes 8 to 10 servings.

TO MAKE SHERRY VINAIGRETTE

Combine oil, sherry vinegar, salt, pepper, maple syrup, and minced serrano, if desired, in a jar with tight-fitting lid or whisk together until salt is dissolved.

Many of these vegetable casserole dishes may be assembled in advance and refrigerated for 1 to 2 days. Bake to finish the dish just before serving. Remove from refrigerator 1 hour before placing in oven. Add about 10 minutes baking time to heat thoroughly.

Corn Casserole

2 (10-ounce) packages frozen whole-kernel corn, thawed and drained
1 (8¾-ounce) can creamed corn
2 eggs, well beaten
½ cup milk or half-and-half
1 teaspoon salt, or to taste
½ teaspoon pepper, or to taste
¼ cup grated Monterey Jack cheese with jalapeños
½ cup crushed cracker crumbs, optional
1 tablespoon butter, melted

Preheat oven to 325°–350°. Lightly coat a 2-quart casserole dish with nonstick cooking spray.

In medium mixing bowl, combine thawed corn, creamed corn, eggs, milk, salt, pepper, and cheese. Stir to blend and pour into prepared casserole dish. Sprinkle top with cracker crumbs, if desired. Drizzle melted butter over top and bake for 30 to 35 minutes or until firm, not runny, in the middle.

Makes 8 to 10 servings.

Baked Winter Squash

3 large (about 3–4 pounds) acorn squash, or other type of winter squash
2 eggs, lightly beaten
½ cup plus 2–3 tablespoons brown sugar (divided use)
2 tablespoons flour
1 teaspoon vanilla
2 tablespoons butter
½ teaspoon nutmeg

½ teaspoon cinnamon
1 teaspoon salt, or to taste
½ teaspoon pepper, or to taste

Preheat oven to 350°. Cut squash in half and scoop out seeds (or strings). Pierce skin side 2 or 3 times with fork. Place cut side down on a baking sheet and bake squash until tender and easily pierced with a fork. Or microwave 4 to 5 minutes or until tender and easily pierced with a fork.

Drain, and allow to cool slightly. With an oven mitt, hold squash halves and scoop pulp into a large mixing bowl. You should have about 3 cups. Discard squash shells.

To squash pulp, add eggs, ½ cup brown sugar, flour, vanilla, butter, nutmeg, cinnamon, salt, and pepper. Using an electric mixer on low speed, blend until smooth. Pour into 2-quart casserole. Sprinkle 2 to 3 tablespoons brown sugar on top. Bake for 30 minutes or until slightly brown around edges.

Makes 8 to 10 servings.

Easy Spinach Casserole

3 (10-ounce) packages frozen chopped spinach
2 tablespoons butter
½ cup onion, chopped fine
1 to 2 cloves garlic, minced
½ cup freshly grated Parmesan cheese (divided use)
1 cup plain Greek yogurt
1 teaspoon salt, or to taste
½ teaspoon pepper, or to taste

Preheat oven to 325°–350°. Cook spinach according to package directions and drain well, first in a colander, pressing with back of spoon to remove excess liquid. Then wrap several layers of paper towels around spinach and squeeze to remove additional liquid.

Combine butter and onion in medium saucepan. Cook until onion is soft. Add garlic and cook a minute or two longer. Remove from heat. Stir in spinach, all but 2 tablespoons

Parmesan cheese, Greek yogurt, and salt and pepper to taste; mix well. Pour into 1½-quart casserole dish. Sprinkle with remaining Parmesan cheese. Cover with foil and bake for 25 to 30 minutes or until light brown and bubbly.

Makes 8 to 10 servings.

Carrots in Cream

1 pound baby carrots
¼ cup cream
½ teaspoon salt, or to taste
¼ teaspoon pepper, or to taste
½ teaspoon sugar, or to taste

In medium saucepan, combine carrots and 1 cup cold water. Place over high heat and bring water to a boil. Reduce heat, cover pan, and cook carrots until tender and easily pierced with a fork, about 10 to 15 minutes.

Drain carrots and rinse with cold water to stop the cooking. If desired, refrigerate until serving time.

In same saucepan, combine cream, salt, pepper, and sugar over medium heat. Cook and stir until sugar melts. Add drained carrots, stirring to coat evenly. Heat through and adjust seasoning to taste.

Makes 8 to 10 servings.

Green Beans with Lemon Brown Butter

1 pound French green beans
3 tablespoons unsalted butter
1 tablespoon lemon juice
1 teaspoon salt, or to taste
½ teaspoon pepper, or to taste
½ cup toasted slivered or sliced almonds, optional

Steam green beans over boiling water until crisp tender, 4 to 6 minutes. Or microwave on high for 4 to 8 minutes, depending on microwave. Place beans in colander and rinse with cold water to stop cooking. At this point, beans may be refrigerated until serving time.

In medium saucepan, melt butter over medium-high heat. When butter begins to bubble, reduce heat to low and continue cooking until butter turns caramel colored and has brown flecks in it. Remove from heat. Stir in lemon juice, salt, and pepper to taste.

Add beans to saucepan, toss to coat evenly, and heat through. Top with toasted almonds, if desired.

Makes 8 servings.

VARIATION

* Cook 4 cups (about 16 ounces) broccoli florets as fresh green beans above, until tender, 6 to 8 minutes. Proceed as above. Add ½ teaspoon grated nutmeg.

Green Beans with Lemon Brown Butter, p. 92

The following recipe is a more contemporary way to prepare fresh broccoli. It may be served hot or at room temperature.

Sautéed Broccoli with Garlic and Red Pepper

2 tablespoons olive oil
4 cloves garlic, peeled and sliced very thin
1 teaspoon dried red pepper flakes or to taste
4 cups (about 16 ounces) broccoli florets and stem pieces, cut same size
salt to taste
fresh ground black pepper to taste

Heat olive oil in a large skillet over medium-low heat. Add the garlic and cook for about 1 minute. Stir in red pepper flakes and broccoli. Toss with the olive oil and garlic until the broccoli turns bright green and begins to soften, 2 to 3 minutes. Season to taste with salt and black pepper. May be served warm or at room temperature.

Makes 8 servings.

No holiday meal at my German grandmother's was complete without turnips. Cream and a little sugar make them a mild yet distinct flavor to add to a holiday table.

Sweet and Creamy Turnips

2 pounds turnips, about 6
1 cup cream
2 tablespoons butter, melted
2 tablespoons sugar
1 teaspoon salt, or to taste
1 teaspoon pepper, or to taste
1 teaspoon nutmeg
¼ cup finely chopped parsley, optional

Preheat oven to 325°–350°. Peel turnips and cut into eighths. Place in a large saucepan with cold water to cover over high heat. When water boils, reduce heat to simmer and cook until turnips are easily pierced with a fork, about 15 minutes.

Drain turnips and place in 2-quart casserole dish. Combine cream, butter, sugar, salt, and pepper. Pour over turnips and toss to evenly coat. Add a bit more cream if needed and adjust seasoning to taste. Sprinkle with nutmeg.

Cover turnips and place in oven until heated through, about 20 minutes. Sprinkle with parsley, if desired.

Makes 8 to 10 servings.

Christmas Sweets

There's simply no sweeter time of year. The cookies of the season are as evocative as some of the other symbols: the decorated tree, garlands of greenery, and nativity scenes. Cakes, candies, and other desserts are also a big part of the holiday celebration. For some Texans, the memory of the big finale to the family dinner is as memorable as the first bike under the tree.

Cookies

Cookies are the currency for one of the most traditional of holiday exchanges. The baking of family favorites—to offer visitors, including Santa, and to give to friends and neighbors—is a big part of the seasonal celebration in many homes. The recipes in this book are some of my favorites, not intended to be an exhaustive list of holiday cookies.

This simple cookie, called a Mexican wedding cookie, is a Texas favorite. An uncomplicated list of ingredients makes for a wonderful holiday mouthful.

CHRISTMAS DESSERT BUFFET MENU

Coconut Cake, 106

German Chocolate Cake with Coconut Pecan Frosting, 103

Divinity, 110

Mexican Wedding Cookies, 96

Fruitcake Nibbles, 109

Pralines, 111

Margarita Balls, 101

White Chocolate Fudge, 151

Mini-Strudels, 57

Eggnog, 118

*Mexican Wedding Cookies
(bottom left), p. 96, (clockwise)
Decorated Sugar Cookies,
p. 97; Killer Cake-Pops by Laura
Williamee, www.killercakepops.
com; Salted Truffle Brownies
from Central Market baking
mix (upper right); Eggnog,
p. 118; Central Market Organic
Chocolate Truffles (center),
p. 239*

Mexican Wedding Cookies

½ cup butter, softened
½ cup powdered sugar (divided use)
1 cup flour
1 teaspoon vanilla
¼ cup finely chopped pecans

Preheat oven to 300°. Using an electric mixer, combine the butter and 2 tablespoons powdered sugar, beating at medium speed until smooth and fluffy.

Sift the flour and blend into butter, mixing thoroughly. Stir in vanilla. Form dough into 1-inch balls and place on an ungreased cookie sheet; use two fingers to flatten slightly.

Bake for 25 to 30 minutes, or until firm and light golden in color. Cool slightly on a rack. Sift remaining powdered sugar. Roll cookies in sifted powdered sugar while still warm.

Makes about 24 cookies.

⁓

These simple sugar cookies are easy to make as pressed cookies, or you may want to roll them and cut into holiday shapes. Few memories are as cherished as making cookies with a mother or grandmother and proudly presenting them to the family.

Old-Fashioned Sugar Cookies

½ cup vegetable shortening
1 cup sugar
1 egg, lightly beaten
1 teaspoon vanilla
¼ cup milk (or water*)
2½ cups flour
2 teaspoons baking powder
¼ teaspoon salt

Preheat oven to 375°. In medium bowl, combine the shortening and the sugar, beating at high speed with an electric mixer. Mixture should be light and fluffy. Add egg and vanilla.

Sift together the flour, baking powder, and salt. Repeat sifting process, then transfer sifted ingredients into mixing bowl with egg and sugar mixture. Gradually add milk (or water) and blend on low speed until ingredients are smooth. (Use water if cookies are planned for a meal which includes meat, to conform to Jewish dietary law.) Chill dough for 1 to 2 hours for easier handling.

SIMPLE COOKIES

Roll dough into 1-inch balls. Place balls on an ungreased cookie sheet 2 inches apart. Press each ball with the bottom of a glass that has been dipped in sugar until cookie is about ¼ inch thick. Dip glass in sugar before flattening each cookie.

Tips: Use a baking-powder can for a cookie cutter when making cookies for mailing. After baking, pack them for mailing in the same can. The cookies will shrink a bit during baking and fit in the container.

Cool cookie sheets between bakes to prevent dough from spreading.

Don't mix different kinds of cookies for storage because this tends to make them all soggy.

Sprinkle lightly with ground nutmeg or cinnamon. If desired, place a perfect pecan half in the center of each. Bake 8 to 10 minutes or until light golden around the edges. Remove from oven and allow to cool until cookies begin to firm up. Remove to a rack to cool completely.

CUT-OUT COOKIES

Break off a third to a fourth of the dough, returning the rest to the refrigerator. Place on a lightly floured board and gently roll to ¼-inch thickness. Using holiday cutters, cut cookies into desired shapes. Using a spatula, carefully transfer to ungreased baking sheet. Decorate as desired with sprinkles or other holiday decorations. Bake 8 to 10 minutes or until light golden around the edges. Remove from oven and allow to cool until cookies begin to firm up. Remove to a rack to cool completely. Decorate as desired with Decorator Frosting for Cookies, other icing (homemade or purchased), colored sugar, or other cookie decorations.

Makes 2½ to 3 dozen cookies.

DECORATOR FROSTING FOR COOKIES

½ cup powdered sugar
2 teaspoons unsalted butter (or margarine*), softened
2 teaspoons milk (or water*)

In small bowl, combine powdered sugar, butter, and milk. Beat at medium speed until smooth. Color as desired with food coloring. Pipe or spread on completely cooled cookies. After decorating, let stand until frosting is set. Store in loosely covered container.

*Jewish dietary law does not allow dairy and meat in the same meal. To serve these cookies with the brisket Hanukkah menu, use nondairy substitutes.

I attribute one of my favorite food quotes to James Beard, who said, "A gourmet who thinks of calories is like a tart who looks at her watch."

—Jeff Blank

These are similar to miniature pecan pie slices—so good and so festive on a Christmas cookie tray.

Pecan Diamonds

½ cup butter, softened
¼ cup granulated sugar
3 eggs (divided use)
1½ teaspoons vanilla (divided use)
1¼ cups all-purpose flour (sift before measuring)
⅛ plus ½ teaspoon salt (divided use)
1½ cups brown sugar
1 cup chopped pecans
2 tablespoons all-purpose flour
½ teaspoon baking powder

Preheat oven to 350°. Grease a 9 × 13-inch baking pan.

In a small bowl, combine butter and sugar, beating on high speed with an electric mixer until light and fluffy. Beat in 1 egg and ½ teaspoon vanilla. Add sifted flour and ⅛ teaspoon salt, in 3 parts, mixing with a spoon or on low speed after each addition.

Using your hands, pat the dough evenly into the prepared pan. Bake about 15 minutes, or until crust is light golden.

Meanwhile, lightly beat 2 eggs in a medium bowl. Add brown sugar, stirring to dissolve. Stir in pecans, 2 tablespoons flour, baking powder, ½ teaspoon salt, and 1 teaspoon vanilla. Spread over crust and return to oven for about 25 minutes.

Remove from oven and cool completely. Cut into 2 × 2-inch diamond shapes or 1 × 2-inch bars.

Makes about 3 to 4 dozen.

These German gingersnaps have a touch of pepper, like the other classic winter cookie, *pfeffernuesse*.

Gingersnaps

2 cups flour
1 teaspoon ginger
1 teaspoon baking powder
1 teaspoon baking soda
¼ teaspoon black pepper
¼ teaspoon salt
¾ cup shortening
1 cup sugar
¼ cup molasses
1 egg, lightly beaten

Preheat oven to 375°. Lightly grease cookie sheet(s). Sift together flour, ginger, baking powder, baking soda, black pepper, and salt. Set aside.

In a large bowl, combine shortening and sugar, beating on high speed with an electric mixer until light and fluffy. Stir in molasses and egg. Blend sifted mixture into creamed mixture, in 3 parts. Stir in or use mixer on low speed. Cover dough and refrigerate for at least an hour, preferably 2 to 3 hours.

Form 1-inch balls and roll in granulated sugar. Place on lightly greased cookie sheet about 2 inches apart. Flatten with the bottom of a glass dipped in sugar to about ¼ inch thick.

If desired, divide dough and roll a portion on lightly floured board ¼ inch thick and cut with cutters, such as classic gingerbread boys or girls. Repeat, using remaining dough. Refrigerate unused portion until ready to shape.

Bake 8 to 10 minutes, or until golden around edges. Remove from pans immediately and cool on wire racks.

Makes about 5 dozen cookies.

One of Texans' favorite flavors is that of the margarita, the lime-based cocktail with salt on the rim of the glass. These cookies, with just a touch of (optional) tequila and orange liqueur, may become one of your holiday traditions after you taste one. But don't just think of them at Christmas. They're a natural for New Year's or with Mexican food, any time you want a light, refreshing two-bite treat.

Margarita Balls

1½ cups pretzel sticks

1 (12-ounce) package vanilla wafers

¾ cup frozen margarita or limeade concentrate, thawed

6 ounces cream cheese, cut into large cubes and softened
at room temperature

1 teaspoon tequila, or to taste, optional

1 teaspoon orange liqueur or orange brandy, or to taste,
optional

rind from 1 lime, grated fine

1 (16-ounce) package confectioners' sugar, or 4 cups

green, red, or white decorator sugar, as desired

lace pretzel sticks in bowl of food processor fitted with knife blade. Process to fine crumbs. Add vanilla wafers and process to fine crumbs.

Add margarita concentrate and cream cheese, pulsing to combine. Add tequila and orange liqueur or brandy, and lime rind. Gradually add confectioners' sugar, pulsing between additions, to combine.

Refrigerate dough in work bowl for an hour or longer, for easier handling. Shape dough into 1-inch balls. After shaping each ball, roll each in decorator sugar. Repeat until all dough is used. Store in an airtight container in refrigerator up to 1 week.

Makes 5 dozen.

When you want a no-fail, hands-on recipe for kids, try Gail Hearn Plummer's Cinnamon Fingers. Little fingers love to shape the dough into "fingers." And they're virtually impossible to mess up. Besides, they taste great. (They're easy enough for adults to make, too.)

One time my kids were making these and decided to try making one big one (about the size of a Gila monster). It didn't bake the same as the little ones, but they sure had fun.

—*Gail Hearn Plummer*

Cinnamon Fingers

1 cup unsalted butter (2 sticks), softened
5 tablespoons plus ½ cup sugar (divided use)
2 cups all-purpose flour (sift after measuring)
1 teaspoon vanilla
¼ teaspoon cinnamon, or to taste

reheat oven to 350°. Combine butter, 5 tablespoons sugar, flour, and vanilla in work bowl of a food processor. Process in short on-off pulses until mixture forms a soft dough.

Shape dough into "pinky fingers," about ½ inch wide and 2 inches long. Place "fingers" on an ungreased cookie sheet and bake 10 to 12 minutes, just until edges turn golden. Be careful not to overbake.

Meanwhile, combine ½ cup sugar and cinnamon, mixing well to distribute cinnamon evenly. Place on a small saucer.

Remove cookies from oven. Allow to cool slightly, then roll in cinnamon sugar to coat evenly. Cool completely on a wire rack.

Makes 2½ dozen.

Cakes, Candies, Pies, and Desserts

Besides cookies, Christmas is a time for cakes, candies, and pies. Desserts sometimes seem like a main course. Many cooks spend hours, even days, making sweet treats for the holiday season. Nowhere is the influence of German immigrants more evident than in some of Texans' favorite cakes, particularly at Christmas.

This was a chocolate favorite at my German grandmother's house for Christmas. Next to her angel food cake, this was one of her best.

German Chocolate Cake with Coconut Pecan Frosting

1 (4-ounce) bar sweet baking chocolate
½ cup boiling water
1 cup butter, softened
2 cups sugar
4 eggs, separated
1 teaspoon vanilla
2½ cups sifted cake flour (sift before measuring)
½ teaspoon salt
1 teaspoon baking soda
1 cup buttermilk

Preheat oven to 350°. Prepare 3 (8- or 9-inch) cake pans. Grease bottom and sides and dust with flour, shaking to remove excess. Or coat bottom and sides with nonstick baking spray.

Off heat, add chocolate to boiling water. Stir until chocolate melts. Allow to cool slightly.

Combine butter and sugar in a large bowl, beating on high speed with an electric mixer until light and fluffy. Add egg yolks, one at a time, mixing well after each addition. Blend in chocolate and vanilla, mixing well.

Stir together flour, salt, and soda. Add to chocolate mixture, alternately with buttermilk, beginning and ending with dry ingredients. Beat until smooth.

Beat egg whites until stiff peaks form. Gently, blend about ¼ of the chocolate batter into the egg whites. Then fold egg whites into the remaining batter. Blend gently until uniform color is achieved.

Divide batter evenly in prepared cake pans. Bake for 30 to 40 minutes or until a toothpick inserted in center comes out clean. Cool in pans on rack for 10 minutes, then turn out and cool completely on rack.

COCONUT PECAN FROSTING

1 cup evaporated milk (not sweetened condensed milk)
1 cup sugar
3 egg yolks, lightly beaten
½ cup unsalted butter
1 teaspoon vanilla
1½ cups flaked coconut
1 cup chopped pecans

Combine evaporated milk, sugar, egg yolks, and butter in a medium saucepan over medium heat. Cook and stir for 12 minutes, or until mixture thickens.

Remove from heat and stir in vanilla, coconut, and pecans. Using a wooden spoon, beat vigorously until mixture is thick enough to spread, about 5 minutes. (Rest your arm when necessary.)

Place 1 chocolate layer on cake plate. Spread thin layer of frosting on top. Add second layer and spread with another thin layer of frosting. Add third layer and spread frosting on top and sides.

Makes 12 to 16 servings.

Made as a year-round treat for afternoon coffee, this German-style coffee cake has particular personal significance because it was always waiting warm when we arrived on Christmas Eve at my grandmother's house. We knew her as MoMo. Her name was Olga Reichle Koch.

It is also wonderful on a holiday morning.

Olga's Coffee Cake

1 package dry yeast
¼ cup lukewarm water
¾ cup milk
½ cup plus 6 tablespoons sugar (divided use)
¼ cup unsalted butter
1 egg, lightly beaten
1 teaspoon salt
3 cups flour
3–4 tablespoons melted butter

Dissolve yeast in warm water, stirring to activate. Set aside. Heat milk until almost boiling; remove from heat. Add ½ cup sugar and ¼ cup butter. Stir to melt and allow mixture to cool to lukewarm, cool enough not to kill the yeast action nor cook the egg. Transfer to a medium mixing bowl.

Add dissolved yeast, egg, and salt to the lukewarm milk mixture. Add flour, 1 cup at a time, mixing well after each addition. Turn out the dough onto lightly floured board. Knead for 5 to 10 minutes until smooth and shiny. If needed, add a bit more flour.

Place the dough in a lightly greased bowl, cover, and let rise in a warm place until doubled in bulk, about 1½ to 2 hours.

Punch down dough and knead gently in bowl. Allow to rest for 5 to 10 minutes.

Divide dough into 3 pieces. Place on lightly floured board and roll out each piece into a circle about ¼ inch thick and 8 to 9 inches in diameter. Place in a greased 8- or 9-inch cake pan. Cover and let rise again until doubled, about 45 to 60 minutes.

Preheat oven to 375°.

Using fingers, make 6 to 8 indentations in top of each cake. Brush top of cakes with melted butter, allowing butter to puddle in each indentation. Sprinkle about 2 tablespoons sugar over top of each cake.

Bake 20 to 25 minutes or until dough begins to brown around the edges. Serve warm or at room temperature.

Makes 3 (8- or 9-inch) coffee cakes.

My favorite childhood Christmas memory is of a clear, cold night, barreling down a two-lane Texas blacktop on the way to my MoMo's in New Ulm, a small German community between Austin and Houston.

As we slowed, entering the town, the single lighted star that decorated the main intersection came into view. That always meant Christmas was finally upon us.

—*Dotty Griffith*

Although probably English in tradition, coconut cake has long been associated with a Southern Christmas. In some homes, the holiday wouldn't be the same without a towering white layer cake with frothy coconut icing.

Coconut Cake

3½ cups sifted cake flour (sift before measuring)
4 teaspoons baking powder
½ plus 1/8 teaspoon salt (divided use)
1 cup unsalted butter, softened
2 cups sifted sugar (sift before measuring)
½ cup milk plus ½ cup coconut milk, or 1 cup milk
2 teaspoons vanilla (divided use)
10 egg whites (divided use)
2 cups sugar (unsifted)
½ teaspoon cream of tartar
⅓ cup water
2 cups (3.5-ounce can) shredded coconut

Preheat oven to 350°. Grease and flour 3 (8- or 9-inch) cake pans. Combine flour with baking powder and ½ teaspoon salt. Sift together twice. Place butter in large mixing bowl. Beat at high speed with electric mixer until butter is creamy. Gradually add 2 cups sugar, beating after each addition. Beat until mixture is light and fluffy.

Add the flour mixture to the butter mixture, alternating with milk/coconut milk, beginning and ending with flour mixture. Add 1 teaspoon vanilla and mix on medium speed until smooth.

Beat 8 egg whites on high speed until stiff peaks form. Gently stir about ¼ of the batter into beaten egg whites. Fold blended egg whites into remaining batter, being careful not to deflate egg whites.

Divide batter between prepared cake pans. Bake about 20 to 23 minutes or until toothpick inserted in center comes out clean. Allow to cool slightly, then invert cake pans on rack and remove pans. Cool cake layers completely before frosting.

TO MAKE FROSTING

Combine 1½ cups sugar, cream of tartar, water, and ⅛ teaspoon salt in large saucepan over medium heat. Cook and stir until sugar is dissolved and mixture boils rapidly. Remove from heat. Begin beating syrup mixture at high speed with an electric mixer. Add remaining 2 egg whites in an even stream, beating constantly. Beat until peaks form. Add 1 teaspoon vanilla and continue beating until stiff enough to hold stiff peaks.

Place 1 cake layer on cake plate. Spread with thin layer of frosting. Sprinkle with ¼ to ⅓ cup shredded coconut. Add second layer and repeat frosting and coconut. Add third layer and frost top and sides with remaining frosting. Cover top and sides with remaining coconut.

Makes 12 to 16 servings.

Just about every region has a version of this cake, but wherever you go, you'll likely find it called the Texas sheet cake. Fine, we'll take credit for this easy snack cake that is ideal for the Christmas season. In the first edition of this book, the recipe just called for "cocoa." In today's more chocolate-conscious world, I prefer a dark cocoa over milk chocolate. But it's still your choice.

This cake is a buffet favorite when cut into bite-size squares.

2 cups sugar
2 cups unbleached flour
1 cup butter
¼ cup cocoa, preferably dark
1 cup water
½ cup buttermilk
2 eggs, lightly beaten
1 teaspoon baking soda
1 teaspoon vanilla

Preheat oven to 400°. Grease a 15 × 10-inch jelly roll or sheet cake pan.

Sift together sugar and flour in a large bowl. Combine butter, cocoa, and water in a saucepan over high heat and bring to a boil. Stir to melt, remove from heat, and pour over dry ingredients, mixing well.

Allow to cool slightly and stir in buttermilk, eggs, baking soda, and vanilla, mixing well.

Pour batter into prepared pan and bake 20 minutes or until edge of cake begins to pull away from the side of the pan. Do not overbake. Cake should have a fudge-like texture. Five minutes before cake is done, prepare the icing.

ICING

½ cup butter
¼ cup cocoa, preferably dark
⅓ cup milk
1 pound powdered sugar
1 teaspoon vanilla
1 cup chopped pecans

Combine butter, cocoa, and milk in medium saucepan. Cook over low heat until butter is melted. Allow liquid to boil. Remove from heat. Add powdered sugar, vanilla, and pecans and beat until icing is smooth and sugar is dissolved. Spread over hot cake as soon as it comes out of the oven, while it is still in the pan.

Makes 15 (3-inch) squares or 30 (1½-inch) "bites."

Texas is the fruitcake capital of the Western world. The granddaddy of them all, the Collin Street Bakery in Corsicana, as well as Eilenberger Bakery (Butternut Baking Co.) in Palestine and Mary of Puddin Hill in Greenville form the Fruitcake Triangle of East Texas. More fruitcakes are baked here than just about anyplace else you can think of.

With all these fruitcakes to choose from, why even consider baking your own? Because it's Christmas. But you don't have to make a whole fruitcake. For a taste, you can make fruitcake nibbles. They're heavy on nuts, lighter on candied fruit.

Fruitcake Nibbles

¾ cup sugar
¼ cup unsalted butter, softened
1 egg
1⅓ cups sifted flour (sift before measuring)
¼ teaspoon cinnamon
¼ teaspoon nutmeg
¼ teaspoon ground cloves
¼ teaspoon baking soda
¼ teaspoon salt
1 cup coarsely chopped pecans
½ cup dried or candied fruit, chopped
2 tablespoons brandy or bourbon

Preheat oven to 350°. Grease and flour 3 baking sheets or allow sheet to cool between batches. Grease and flour baking sheet each time before forming cookies.

In a medium mixing bowl, beat together sugar, butter, and egg. Sift flour, cinnamon, nutmeg, cloves, baking soda, and salt into bowl. Mix by hand until blended. Add nuts, fruit, and brandy or bourbon. Stir to blend. Batter will be stiff.

Drop dough by rounded teaspoonfuls onto baking sheet. Bake for 12 to 15 minutes, or until golden, about 1 inch apart. If desired, line miniature muffin cups with muffin liners and fill three-quarters full.

Makes about 3 dozen cookies.

The yin and yang of Texas Christmas candies are Chocolate Peppermint Fudge (see p. 150) and divinity. With or without nuts, usually pecans, divinity, as white and fluffy as fudge is dark and dense, is the perfect yang to chocolate's yin. A true Texas holiday candy maker does both.

Divinity

2¾ cups sugar (divided use)
¾ cup white corn syrup
¼ cup water
2 egg whites
1 teaspoon vanilla
1 cup coarsely chopped pecans

Combine 2½ cups sugar, corn syrup, and water in a saucepan over medium heat. Bring to a boil, stirring constantly. When mixture boils, continue cooking at a boil and without stirring until mixture reaches 250° on a candy thermometer. Remove from heat.

Place egg whites in medium bowl. With electric mixer, begin beating egg whites. When egg whites are foamy, gradually add ¼ cup sugar, beating continuously until egg whites form stiff peaks. Pour the boiled mixture slowly into the egg whites, beating constantly on high speed with electric beaters. Stir in vanilla and chopped pecans.

Working quickly, drop candy by teaspoonfuls onto wax paper and cool. Store in airtight containers.

Makes 3½ dozen.

You've probably enjoyed pralines in Tex-Mex restaurants. There's usually a platterful at the cash register. So rich, so monstrous, so chock full of nuts, you wonder why they're the perfect ending to a meal as big as an Enchilada Special. No one knows why. They just are. And they're also very much a Texas tradition at Christmas, for giving or having on hand.

Tip: This confection can be tricky on humid days. The candy just won't "set up," or firm enough to hold a shape. Never mind if it flattens to little patties. Give it a day to dry out, then shape the patties into mounds. They'll be just fine.

Pralines

- 2 cups sugar
- ¾ cup milk
- ¼ teaspoon baking soda
- 1 teaspoon butter
- 1 teaspoon vanilla
- 1½ cups shelled pecan halves or broken pecan pieces

In a large saucepan, combine sugar, milk, and baking soda. Cook over high heat, stirring constantly. Bring mixture to a boil. Continue boiling and stirring until it reaches 240° on a candy thermometer (soft-ball stage).

Remove from heat and add butter, vanilla, and pecans. Using a wooden spoon, beat until mixture begins to hold a shape. Drop by tablespoonfuls onto lightly greased or buttered wax paper.

Makes 1½ dozen.

My very German grandmother (MoMo) on my mother's side and my very Southern grandmother (Netta Morrill Griffith, we called her Netsie Mother) on my dad's side had at least one thing in common around Christmas: mincemeat pie with eggnog. Again, this is likely an English tradition via the Old South.

I can't say the pie was my favorite as a kid, but it was a custom that insinuated itself into the celebrations of those two families from very different backgrounds.

Both relied on prepared mincemeat, which doesn't contain any meat. It is raisins, dates, and similar dried fruit. It is something grandmothers love.

Mince-Apple Pie

- 3 cups apple, peeled and sliced
- ¼ cup sugar
- 1 tablespoon flour
- 1 (28-ounce) jar prepared mincemeat
- 3 tablespoons bourbon, brandy, or orange juice
- pastry for 2-crust pie, see p. 33–34

reheat oven to 450°. Toss together apples, sugar, and flour. Fold into mincemeat, along with bourbon, brandy, or juice.

Line bottom of 9-inch pie plate with bottom crust. Fill with mincemeat filling. Cover the pie with a layer of pastry. Seal and flute edges. Prick top with fork. Decorate as desired with pastry.

Bake for 10 minutes, then lower heat to 350°. Bake about 30 minutes longer, until pastry is golden. Serve warm with a dollop of vanilla ice cream, or at room temperature with whipped cream.

Makes 8 servings.

Mince pies in Ireland are as much a part of Christmas as Midnight Mass, spiced beef, and the Christmas turkey. Omitting them now, just because I live in Texas, would be gross negligence on my part! These melt-in-your-mouth sweets are part of my Texas Christmas tradition. These are best served warm with freshly whipped cream, vanilla ice cream, or my personal favorite, brandy butter.

—Rachel Gaffney

achel Gaffney is Irish by birth, Texan for a decade or so. She and her family have been part of our holiday table for a number of years. She's made mincemeat lovers out of all of us with these individual tarts.

Rachel recommends using King Arthur unbleached flour, Crosse & Blackwell mincemeat, and Kerrygold Pure Irish Butter. Well, of course she does; and she's right. Rachel teaches Irish cooking classes, blogs on Irish cooking (http://rachelgaffney .blogspot.com), and leads trips to Ireland.

Mini-Mince Pies

2 cups all-purpose flour
½ teaspoon salt
¾ cup (12 tablespoons) unsalted butter, cut into cubes
6 to 10 teaspoons ice-cold water
1 egg
scant 1 tablespoon milk
1 (20.5-ounce) jar prepared mincemeat

Preheat oven to 425°. Grease bottom and sides of 12-cupcake pan. Have ready 2 round cookie cutters, 3½ and 3 inches in diameter with fluted edges.

In a food processor, pulse to combine flour and salt. Add butter, pulsing until mixture resembles coarse meal. Add water, 1 teaspoon at a time, pulsing after each addition, until dough begins to form a ball. Wrap dough in plastic wrap and refrigerate an hour for easier handling. Sprinkle countertop or surface of large board with flour and roll out dough to ⅛-inch thickness, as for pie crust.

Using 3½-inch cookie cutter cut out 12 bottom crusts and fit onto bottom and sides of each cup in the pan. Reserve remaining dough.

Spoon a generous ⅓ cup mincemeat into the center of each pie. If needed, reroll dough as before and use the 3-inch cookie cutter to cut 12 tops for the pies. Use a fork to crimp edges together and seal.

Beat together egg and milk. Using a pastry brush, brush the top of each pie with egg-milk mixture. With a fork, prick the top crust of each mince pie once in the center. Bake for about 20 minutes or until edges are golden. Let cool on a baking rack.

Serve with Brandy Butter: In mixer bowl, cream together ½ cup (8 tablespoons) unsalted butter, softened at room temperature, with 8 ounces (2 cups) confectioners' sugar. Stir in 2 tablespoons of brandy. The brandy butter may be made in advance and refrigerated for up to 2 weeks.

Makes 2 dozen.

While tamales are almost always present on holiday tables in households with Mexican origins, a special kind of tamale shows up at Christmas: the sweet tamale. The tamale dough is flavored with cinnamon and sugar; then it is filled with pecans and raisins. Sweet tamales are particularly good with hot chocolate.

5 cups masa harina (found alongside flour and cornmeal in
   the supermarket)
2 teaspoons salt, or to taste
1 teaspoon baking powder
1 tablespoon cinnamon
½ cup sugar
1 cup lard (no substitutes)
3 cups (approximately) chicken stock, heated
⅔ cup pecans, coarsely chopped
3 dozen corn husks, rinsed and soaked in hot water for
   several hours to soften
¾ cup raisins

TO PREPARE THE DOUGH

Combine masa harina, salt, baking powder, cinnamon, and sugar; set aside. Place lard in a large mixing bowl and beat at high speed with an electric beater until light and fluffy, about 3 to 5 minutes. Add masa mixture in 2 to 3 batches, alternately with the warm (not hot) stock, beating constantly. Add nuts, mixing to distribute evenly through the dough.

Dough should be soft, but pliable, not watery. To test dough, place a small piece in a cup of water. If the dough floats, it is the right consistency.

TO SHAPE AND WRAP TAMALES

Pat dry the corn husks. Wet your hands. Place a husk in the palm of one hand, and using the back of a spoon, spread about 2 tablespoons of the dough into a rectangle, starting at the wide end of the shuck. Leave about 1½ inches at the wide end of the shuck and about 3 inches at the pointed end. Spread dough to within ¾ inch of the sides.

Fill with 1 teaspoon raisins. Roll sides of tamales to seal the filling. Fold over wide end to seal bottom. Place folded side down on cookie sheet or large sheet of foil. Repeat until dough and filling are used. You should have about 2 dozen.

Mexican Hot Chocolate, p. 116;
Sweet Tamales, p. 114

TO STEAM

Use a large tamale steamer or large pot with a rack or colander in the bottom. Fill bottom with water to depth of about 1 inch. Water should not touch the rack. Line rack with some of the remaining shucks. Arrange tamales vertically—wide, folded end down—on rack. Tamales should be packed, but not crammed, so they will remain vertical. Cover the tamales with more corn husks or a layer of clean dish towels to prevent the tamales from absorbing too much water. They should be steamed, not immersed. Cover pot with lid.

Bring water to a boil, reduce heat, and simmer for 1½ hours. Make sure water does not cook away during this time; add more as needed. Check tamales for doneness. Tamales are done when the masa easily separates from the husk and the tamale retains its shape. If not done, continue steaming for up to 2½ hours, or as needed. If necessary, cook tamales in batches, reserving tamales in refrigerator until ready to cook.

Cooked tamales may be refrigerated several days or frozen for several weeks. Reheat, wrapped tightly in foil, in a 300° oven, about 30 minutes.

Makes about 2 dozen.

Mexican Hot Chocolate

3 (1-ounce) squares unsweetened chocolate
6 cups milk
¼ cup sugar
2 teaspoons ground cinnamon
¼ teaspoon salt
2 teaspoons vanilla
6 cinnamon sticks, optional

Using a sharp knife, break up chocolate squares into smaller pieces. In a medium saucepan, combine chocolate, milk, sugar, cinnamon, and salt. Heat and stir until chocolate melts and milk is very hot. Do not allow to boil. Add vanilla and beat until frothy with a rotary beater or with an electric mixer on low speed.

Pour into mugs. Garnish each with a cinnamon stick.

Makes 6 (8-ounce) servings.

Other Tex-Mex holiday traditions are sweet, such as flan. This caramel custard is a beautiful dessert for any meal. It is easier to caramelize the sugar in the same pan in which you bake the flan. Use a 9-inch cake pan, a tart pan, or ring mold. The pan must be able to withstand stovetop heat. Use heavy oven mitts to handle.

You may also caramelize the sugar in a small saucepan or skillet and quickly pour into a glass pie plate or porcelain quiche plate for baking flan.

Flan

1½ cups sugar (divided use)
5 eggs, well beaten
1 (13-ounce) can evaporated milk
1 cup heavy cream
2 teaspoons vanilla

Preheat oven to 325°. Sprinkle ½ cup sugar over bottom of a 9-inch cake or pie pan and place over medium heat. Cook, stirring constantly, until sugar melts and turns golden brown. Remove from heat. Turn pan to coat bottom and sides evenly. Allow to cool.

In a medium mixing bowl, combine 1 cup sugar, eggs, evaporated milk, cream, and vanilla, blending well. Pour over caramel in pan. Place pan with flan in a larger shallow pan.

Place in oven. Pour enough hot water into larger pan to come up the side of flan pan about 1 inch. Bake for 55 to 60 minutes, or until a knife inserted near the center comes out clean. Center will jiggle but not appear fluid.

Remove from oven and lift flan pan from water. Cool for 10 to 15 minutes. Invert onto a serving dish with a rim. The caramel will form a sauce on top of the baked custard.

Garnish with Candied Cranberries (see p. 119) if desired.

Makes 8 servings.

The punch bowls of England and the hospitality of the Old South bring to mind the rich Christmas beverage we know as eggnog. This version, using a boiled custard, has scant resemblance to gooey commercially prepared eggnog available in refrigerator cases. This is lighter, much more like a milk punch.

With spirits added, this punch can be potent. Of course, it can be served without.

Make two batches of eggnog, one with and the other without spirits for kids and those who don't imbibe. Make sure guests know they have an option.

Eggnog

⅔ cup sugar

4 egg yolks (reserve whites for another use or discard)

½ teaspoon salt

8 cups milk

1 tablespoon vanilla

1 cup bourbon, dark rum, or brandy (or a combination to make 1 cup), optional or to taste

1 cup whipping cream

ground nutmeg

In large saucepan, combine sugar and egg yolks. Beat until smooth and light yellow in color. Add salt and stir in milk. Cook over medium heat, stirring constantly, until mixture bubbles and thickens enough to coat the back of a spoon.

Remove from heat and stir in vanilla. Place custard in rigid refrigerator container or pitcher with lid. Stir in spirits, if desired. Place a layer of plastic wrap directly on custard. Place lid on container and refrigerate to cool completely, 3 to 4 hours.

Just before serving, whip cream until peaks form. Pour chilled eggnog into a chilled punch bowl and garnish with dollops of whipped cream floating on top. Sprinkle with nutmeg.

Makes 6 to 8 servings.

Holidays in Texas evoke an excitement in my body and soul. I nourish myself with feast, festivity, fellowship, flavor, family, Father, and new focus. Long live the Texas foods of the holidays!

—Susan Teepler Auler

These are a beautiful garnish for holiday desserts, pies, cakes, or tarts or as a sweet-tart addition to a salad. A by-product is a beautiful pink, simple syrup which can be used in various ways including cocktails, tea, and fruit salads.

Candied Cranberries and Cranberry Syrup

2 cups sugar
½ cup water
1 cup fresh cranberries

Place sugar and water in a small saucepan over high heat. Bring to a boil and add cranberries. Cook just until cranberries begin to pop. Remove cranberries with a slotted spoon to plate, spreading in a single layer to dry.

Reserve cranberry syrup for desserts or holiday pancakes.

Makes 1 cup candied cranberries; about 2 cups cranberry syrup.

Texas Lamb Lollipops with Cilantro Mint Pesto, p. 127; (clockwise) Black-Eyed Pea Jalapeño Fritters, p. 122, with Roasted Red Pepper Coulis, p. 123; and Creamy Green Chile Dressing, p. 123; Merry Tomatoes, 125; Gulf Coast Oyster Stew, p. 68, and mug prepped for Gulf Coast Oyster Stew-ters, p. 125; East Texas "Polenta" with Black-Eyed Pea Top-enade, p. 124

New Year's

New Year's Eve

New Year's Eve is party time in Texas. There are two ways to go: Texas fancy or casual.

Nothing says party in this state like nachos, an assortment of dips (including guacamole), margaritas, and a cooler full of Texas and Mexican beers. If that doesn't make you yearn for a steaming bowl of posole on New Year's Day, you won't need it.

Or consider a cocktail buffet with iced Texas vodka or champagne. Trendy noshes like lamb chop lollipops, wild mushroom strudel, and black-eyed pea fritters fulfill the requirements for fun finger food with a nod toward culinary fashion.

While tradition often dictates the menu on other holidays, superstition is the main ingredient for ringing in a new year. Eating black-eyed peas is as much a requirement for a Texas New Year as rice is for a Chinese New Year. You can dress 'em up or go traditional. No matter whether you're going casual or more formal, black-eyed peas in some form are de rigeur for luck in the new year.

One way to get everyone to eat a lucky bite is to serve black-eyed pea fritters. They look like meatballs but are a great vegetarian and gluten free nosh on a buffet table. Make sure your guests know this is the option for those who limit their diets thusly. I added this version in honor of my son Kelly's Peace Corps service in The Gambia, West Africa. When I visited him we ate black-eyed peas lots of different ways. Fritters like these are popular in many part of Africa, where they are known by a number of names: *accra*, *akara*, *akla*, *binch akara*, bean balls, *kosai*, *koose*, *kose*, *koosé*, and *kwasi*, depending on where you are and who is making them.

Best to start the fritters a day ahead because the dried peas must soak several hours or overnight to soften. If time allows, it's even better if you can let the batter "set up" in the refrigerator for several hours, even overnight.

It is okay to fry the fritters a few hours in advance. Refrigerate until ready to reheat in 300° F oven until hot, about 10 minutes.

Champagne

Variety of Texas spirit cocktails, 215

Merry Tomatoes, 125

East Texas "Polenta" with Black-Eyed Pea Top-enade, 124

Black-Eyed Pea Jalapeño Fritters, 122

with Roasted Red Pepper Coulis, 123

and Creamy Green Chile Dressing, 123

Wild Mushroom Strudel, 126

Gulf Coast Oyster Stew-ters, 125

Texas Lamb Lollipops with Cilantro Mint Pesto, 127

CASUAL NEW YEAR'S EVE MENU

Margaritas, 220

Variety of Texas craft beers, 213

Chile con Queso, 130

Guacamole, 131

Salsa, 160

and tortilla chips

Lone Star Caviar (Black-Eyed Pea Relish), 155

Smoked Turkey, 11

and Biscuits, 75

Texas Sheet Cake, 108

Black-Eyed Pea Jalapeño Fritters

½ pound dried black-eyed peas
1 egg, lightly beaten
3 tablespoons cornmeal
4 cloves garlic
2 teaspoon cumin
1 teaspoon salt, or to taste
½ teaspoon freshly ground black pepper, or to taste
½ teaspoon cayenne pepper, or to taste
4 to 6 tablespoons water
½ cup coarse chopped onion
2 small fresh jalapeños, stemmed and ribbed, coarsely chopped
1 teaspoon fresh minced ginger
peanut oil for frying
salt to taste
pieces of fresh lime to squeeze on the fritters

Place dried peas in a colander and rinse several times. Place in a large bowl and cover with cold water. Soak several hours or overnight until peas soften. Rinse several times.

Place drained peas in the bowl of a food processor fitted with metal blade. Add egg, cornmeal, garlic, cumin, salt, pepper, and cayenne. Pulse to blend. With the motor running, slowly add water and continue processing to make a smooth, thick batter. The batter should be thick enough to cling to a spoon. Add onion, jalapeño, and ginger; pulse several times to finely chop vegetables and blend into the batter. Refrigerate several hours or overnight so the batter firms.

When ready to fry, heat 2 to 3 inches of peanut oil in a large skillet or deep fryer to 375°. Drop mixture by tablespoonfuls into the hot oil a few at a time. Fry until golden brown on all sides, 2 to 3 minutes, turning with a slotted spoon. Drain on paper towels. Serve hot, sprinkled with salt and lime juice.

Makes 40 pieces.

This is a riff on ranch dressing using Greek yogurt. Use it as a salad dressing or a dip for veggies or black-eyed pea fritters.

Creamy Green Chile Dressing

1 cup plain Greek yogurt
½ cup mayonnaise
¼ cup chopped cilantro
½ cup finely chopped green onions, white part only
1 clove garlic, peeled
½ teaspoon coarse sea salt
¼ to ½ cup cold buttermilk
salt and coarse ground black pepper to taste
½ cup chopped roasted green chile, or to taste

In a medium bowl, stir together Greek yogurt, mayonnaise, cilantro, and green onion. On a cutting board, smash a whole garlic clove using the flat part of a knife blade. Sprinkle garlic with about ½ teaspoon coarse sea salt. With a fork, smash the salt into the garlic to create a paste.

Stir garlic paste into dressing. Gradually whisk in buttermilk to desired consistency; thicker for dipping sauce, thinner for salad dressing. Add salt and pepper to taste; fold in chopped green chile.

Place dressing in an airtight container and refrigerate for several hours to let flavors meld. Refrigerate up to 1 week.

Makes about 2½ cups dressing.

This is almost as easy to prepare as it is to buy. So you decide.

Roasted Red Pepper Coulis

1 (12-ounce) jar roasted red peppers, drained
3 tablespoons extra-virgin olive oil
1 medium shallot, thinly sliced
1 tablespoon sherry vinegar
salt and freshly ground white pepper to taste

Place the peppers, olive oil, shallot, and vinegar into work bowl of a food processor or blender. Puree until very smooth. Season with salt and white pepper.

The coulis can be refrigerated overnight. Bring to room temperature before serving.

Makes ¾ to 1 cup.

This dish combines several recipes from various chapters to make a rustic pickup nosh. Here's the deal: prepared silver-dollar-size fried cornmeal cakes (p. 144), which I'm fancying up in this chapter with the name East Texas "Polenta." Top with a schmear of Canyon Foods Sweet Chile Lime Sauce–laced cream cheese and Lone Star Caviar. Add a dot of crèma (Mexican-style crème fraiche) if you like.

East Texas "Polenta" with Black-Eyed Pea Top-enade

2 dozen fried cornmeal rounds made from Hot Water Corn Bread (p. 144)
6 ounces cream cheese, softened at room temperature
¼ cup Canyon Foods Sweet Chile Lime Sauce or favorite flavor sauce such as Sriracha or red pepper sauce (to taste)
milk or cream, optional
2 cups Lone Star Caviar (p. 155), drained to remove excess dressing
crema, optional

Prepare cornmeal and shape into bite-size rounds, 1 to 2 inches in diameter. These may be fried a day ahead. Cover to prevent drying. Serve at room temperature.

Combine cream cheese with Canyon Foods Sweet Chile Lime Sauce in a small bowl. Or substitute your favorite prepared sauce. It could be anything from steak or barbecue sauce to a thick salad dressing. May also use milk or cream to whip with cream cheese to achieve spreadable consistency.

Use an electric mixer to mix sauce with cream cheese until smooth and fluffy. Add milk or cream, if desired, to achieve soft, smooth consistency.

To assemble, spread a generous amount of cream cheese on each cornmeal round. Or use a pastry bag and pipe a dollop on to each "polenta" round. Top with a spoonful of Lone Star Caviar. Place on serving tray. If desired, top with a dot of crema, applied with a squirt bottle.

Makes 24 hors d'oeuvres.

*F*riend and caterer Michael Burke says you won't believe how something this simple "just flies off the cocktail buffet table." Serve with plenty of toothpicks so guests may skewer a vodka "merrynated" tomato and dip it into the dry seasoning blend.

Merry Tomatoes

1 pint grape tomatoes (approximately 38 tomatoes)
½ cup vodka or as needed
½ cup your favorite brand lemon seasoning blend
2 tablespoons celery salt
cracked black pepper to taste
2 teaspoons curry powder or to taste

*R*inse tomatoes and place in a shallow serving bowl. Pour vodka over tomatoes using enough until tomatoes are, at least, partially submerged.

In small bowl or shaker, combine lemon seasoning blend, celery salt, cracked black pepper, and curry power. Stir or cover tightly and shake to combine. Transfer to small serving dish.

Serve tomatoes with plenty of toothpicks.

About 6 servings.

Tip: These tomatoes look beautiful on a buffet presented in an oversize martini glass. Serve seasoning blend in a small ramekin for dipping. Make sure there are plenty of toothpicks for spearing tomatoes.

*T*his is a take on popular shooters, individual servings that can be sipped or spooned from a shot glass or other small container. This party version is fun and interactive as well as delicious for true oyster lovers.

Gulf Coast Oyster Stew-ters

ingredients for Gulf Coast Oyster Stew (p. 68)
24 small oysters with their liquor (about 1 pint)
24 (½-teaspoon) dabs of butter
favorite Louisiana-style hot sauce
finely chopped green onions

*P*repare the liquid for the stew without the oysters. This may be done ahead of time and reheated. Serve very hot.

To assemble stew-ters, place an oyster and a bit of oyster liquor in each of 2 dozen small (4-ounce) shot or juice glasses. Top each with a dab of butter, a generous shot of hot sauce, and a sprinkling of chopped green onions.

Place on serving tray alongside a soup tureen or carafe of very hot stew liquid. Pour a ladleful of hot stew over the oyster. Serve and eat immediately. Guests may prepare their own. Do not allow fresh oysters to sit out unrefrigerated for more than 15 minutes.

Makes 24 hors d'oeuvre servings.

My friend, Karen Cassady, coordinator of cooking schools at Central Market, swears by this recipe, which she says students declare a major winner.

Wild Mushroom Strudel

28 ounces mixed shiitake, oyster, cremini, portobello, and white mushrooms
1 shallot, chopped
2 cloves garlic, minced
1 tablespoon chopped fresh basil
3 teaspoons chopped fresh thyme (divided use)
½ cup butter (divided use)
¼ cup pine nuts, toasted
salt and pepper to taste
8 sheets phyllo pastry

Clean, trim, and coarsely slice the mushrooms. In a skillet over medium heat, sauté shallots, garlic, basil, and 2 teaspoons thyme in 3 tablespoons butter until garlic is soft. Add mushrooms and sauté 15 minutes until mushrooms are very tender. Stir in pine nuts and season to taste with salt and pepper.

Layer 2 sheets of phyllo on a kitchen towel on a flat surface; cover the remaining phyllo with plastic wrap and a damp towel.

Brush the phyllo with some of the melted butter and top with 2 phyllo sheets. Brush with butter and sprinkle with half the remaining 1 teaspoon thyme. Top with the remaining phyllo sheets and brush with butter.

Spoon the mushroom mixture in a line 2 inches from the long edge, leaving a 2-inch edge at the top and bottom. Fold the narrow edges over the filling and brush with butter.

Roll the phyllo to enclose the filling, starting at the long edge closest to the filling and lifting the towel to help roll. Lift the roll with a spatula and place seam side down on a buttered baking sheet. Place in the freezer for 5 minutes.

Preheat oven to 350°.

Remove strudel from freezer and brush with butter. Bake for 15 minutes or until golden brown. Cut into slices to serve.

Makes 8 appetizer servings; 4 main dish servings.

⁓

My oft-mentioned friend and caterer, Michael Burke, serves these for party buffets. Allow at least 2 chops per guest.

Texas Lamb Lollipops with Cilantro Mint Pesto

16 lamb chops (about 2 racks), Frenched (rib bones exposed in the French style)* and lollipopped*
½ cup olive oil
¼ cup soy sauce
1 teaspoon minced fresh ginger
Cilantro Mint Pesto (see below)
3 to 4 fresh garlic cloves, ends trimmed
salt and pepper to taste

Trim lamb chops as needed to make neat "lollipops": rib bones exposed, with medallions of lamb loin on the bone. Place lamb chops in 1 or 2 large resealable plastic bags. Combine olive oil, soy sauce, and ginger. Pour over lamb. Rub marinade into chops to coat evenly. Refrigerate, turning once or twice,

Tip: Purchase 2 racks of lamb (a rack typically has 7 or 8 ribs) with the bones "Frenched" or trimmed and skinned. Cut between the ribs to separate into chops. Or have a butcher cut chops into "lollipops" by Frenching the ribs and removing excess fat to leave a medallion of lamb loin on each rib.

several hours or preferably overnight. Prepare and reserve Cilantro Mint Pesto.

Remove chops from refrigerator an hour before ready to grill or roast. Prepare medium hot coals or preheat oven to 375°F.

Rub chops with cut ends of fresh garlic. Season with salt and pepper to taste. Grill or roast chops to rare, about 10 to 15 minutes. Keep warm until ready to serve. If serving immediately, grill or roast to medium rare.

Serve with Cilantro Mint Pesto.

Makes 8 servings (2 chops per person).

CILANTRO MINT PESTO

> 1 cup loosely packed cilantro leaves
> ½ cup loosely packed mint leaves
> 1 bunch scallions, trimmed and white part cut into several pieces
> ½ cup pine nuts, toasted*
> 1 cup extra-virgin olive oil
> ¼ cup white balsamic vinegar
> salt and pepper to taste

To toast pine nuts: place nuts in a dry skillet and cook over medium-low heat, stirring frequently, until golden in spots, about 3 minutes. Allow to cool.

Place cilantro and mint leaves in food processor or blender, along with pieces of scallion. Add toasted pine nuts, olive oil, vinegar, and salt and pepper to taste. Process or blend until smooth. Store in refrigerator. Allow to come to room temperature before serving.

Makes 2½ cups.

Nachos, a snack said to have originated in the border town of Piedras Negras, can be as simple as cheese melted on chips with a slice of jalapeño. Indeed, that is the dish attributed to a waiter named "Nacho." Or nachos can be more elaborate, with a smear of refried beans, and a mouthful of beef or chicken. Garnishes can be many and varied, such as guacamole, sour cream, and Pico de Gallo (see p. 160).

Nachos

1 (24-ounce) bag restaurant-style tortilla chips
1 (16-ounce) package grated cheddar cheese
1 (12-ounce) jar or can sliced jalapeños
1 (16-ounce) can refried beans, optional
½ pound ground beef, cooked, optional
2 cups shredded, cooked chicken, optional
1 cup Guacamole, optional (p. 131)
1 cup sour cream, optional
½ cup Pico de Gallo, optional (p. 160)
1 cup rings sliced from a large onion, optional

Preheat broiler. Arrange tortilla chips in a single layer on several baking sheets. For basic nachos, top with a sprinkle of grated cheese and a jalapeño slice. If mild nachos are desired, omit some or all of the jalapeño slices and serve as a garnish. Place nachos under broiler just until cheese melts, 3 to 5 minutes.

Makes 8 to 10 servings.

OPTIONS

* Spread each chip with refried beans before topping with cheese and pepper. Proceed as above.
* Cook ground beef in a skillet over medium heat until brown. Drain off fat. Add 1 tablespoon chili powder and 1 tablespoon water, stirring well. Cook 5 minutes longer. Place a teaspoon of ground beef on top of each chip. Top with cheese. Add jalapeños as desired. Proceed as above.
* Shred chicken and place a tablespoon on top of each chip. Top with cheese. Add jalapeños as desired. Proceed as above.
* After removing nachos from oven, garnish every other nacho or so with a teaspoon of Guacamole, or arrange ¼-cup dollops strategically around nacho platter.
* After removing nachos from oven, garnish every other nacho or so with a teaspoon of sour cream, or arrange ¼-cup dollops strategically around nacho platter.

Tip: For killer nachos, make them with the works—some of everything: cheese, jalapeños, beans, beef, chicken, guacamole, sour cream, and pico de gallo. Offer plenty of Salsa (p. 161) and Chile con Queso (p. 130), as well. Nachos like that are a meal, not a snack.

* Omit onions. Combine
processed cheese with
tomatoes and green
chilies and chicken stock
in a 2-quart microwave-
safe dish. Microwave on
high for 3 minutes; stir.
Continue microwaving,
stirring at a 1-minute
intervals, until cheese is
melted.

* Omit onions and
chicken stock. Combine
processed cheese with
undrained tomatoes and
green chilies or 1 cup
bottled salsa in a 2-quart
microwave-safe dish.
Follow above instructions
for heating in microwave.

* Omit onions. Combine
cheese, chicken stock,
and drained tomatoes
and green chilies, or
undrained tomatoes
and green chilies, in
a stockpot. Heat on
high until cheese melts.
Add chicken stock if
additional liquid is
needed. Keep warm on
low setting.

* Brown and drain fat from
1 cup ground beef, bulk
pork, venison or Italian
sausage, or chorizo
(Mexican sausage), or
shred 1 cup leftover
barbecued brisket or
chicken and add to Chile
con Queso just before
serving.

* After removing nachos from oven, garnish every other nacho or so with a teaspoon of Pico de Gallo, or arrange ¼-cup dollops strategically around nacho platter.
* After removing nachos from oven, garnish with fresh onion rings.

The late Matt Martinez, a legendary character and Dallas chef-restaurateur, always swore the key to a great chile con queso was a bit of chicken stock. He was, of course, right. Chicken stock mellows the taste of the cheese and gives it a smoother texture that doesn't get gooey.

Chile con Queso

½ cup onion, coarsely chopped
½–¾ cup chicken stock, or as needed (divided use)
1 (10-ounce) can tomatoes with green chilies
1 (16-ounce) block of processed cheese,
cut in 2-inch cubes

Place onion in a large saucepan over low heat. Add 1 tablespoon chicken stock and cook until onion begins to soften, 2 to 3 minutes. Stir in tomatoes and cheese. As cheese begins to melt, stir in chicken stock, ¼ cup at a time, until cheese is melted. Add chicken stock as needed for desired consistency.

Use minimum chicken stock to make a thick sauce for dipping tortilla chips. Add more stock for a thinner consistency to use as a sauce for spooning over other dishes, such as enchiladas.

This recipe reheats with great success; can be made in slow cooker.

Makes about 4 cups.

In Texas, all that's required for a party are two friends, chips, chile con queso, and guacamole. Adult beverages are optional, but customary. There's simply nothing better.

This version of guacamole is the bare basics, mostly avocado.

Guacamole

3 large ripe avocados (about 3 cups)
½ cup finely chopped onion
1 teaspoon salt, or to taste
juice of ½ lemon or lime, or to taste

Peel avocados and place pulp in a medium bowl. Use a fork or potato masher to coarsely mash. Add onion, salt, and lemon or lime juice. Stir and mash again to desired consistency. Mixture should not be too smooth. Serve immediately as a dip for tortilla chips or as a garnish for nachos or enchiladas.

Optional add-ins: 1 small jalapeño, seeded and finely chopped; 2 to 3 tablespoons chopped cilantro; 2 to 3 tablespoons finely chopped tomato (no seeds).

Makes 3 cups.

Tip: To keep guacamole from turning brown, place plastic wrap directly on the dip, sealing at the edges, to keep out as much air as possible. If guacamole oxidizes on top, carefully scrape away the brown layer, for appearance's sake.

New Year's Day

For many Texans, football is as much a part of New Year's Day as Thanksgiving Day. Although the Super Bowl isn't played until later in January or early February, many Texans get a head start with a super bowl of black-eyed peas, chili, gumbo, posole, or tortilla soup. Barbecue—beef, ribs, sausage, or a combination—also makes a great spread. It is classic casual food for eating whenever the mood strikes or during commercials. Often

Martinez-Style Smoked Brisket, p. 133; Barbecue Sauce, p. 134; Buzz's Pot of Beans, p. 141

barbecue is brought home from a favorite neighborhood smoke-house, but a lot of Texans take pride in their homemade barbe-cue. For those determined do-it-yourselfers, here's how.

My friend, the late Matt Martinez, made it his mission in life to develop techniques for nonprofessional barbecue cooks to make barbecue as good as that of pitmasters with big rigs. He told me about this technique. It gives a good smoke flavor to the meat without the hassle of minding a smoker. Have ready a squirt gun to douse any flames that might flare when the fat hits the fire.

Martinez-Style Smoked Brisket

1 (8–10-pound) whole beef brisket, with fat layer
 untrimmed
2 tablespoons garlic salt
2 tablespoons lemon pepper
2 tablespoons paprika
1 tablespoon chili powder
1 tablespoon sugar

Remove brisket from refrigerator about 1 hour before grilling. Combine garlic salt, lemon pepper, paprika, chili powder, and sugar. Sprinkle over entire surface of meat, concentrating on the fat layer. Rub or press seasoning into meat.

Cover and let meat come to room temperature. Light a fire in a charcoal grill that is big enough to hold the brisket. Allow coals to burn down to gray ash. Place brisket on grill, fat side down.

Grill until fat is charred, turning occasionally when necessary, to stop fat from dripping onto fire. Squirt flare-ups with water to douse flames.

It will take about 45 minutes to grill the brisket. Remove brisket from grill.

Preheat oven to 300°. Place brisket on a double thickness of foil in a shallow roasting pan. Wrap brisket tightly and bake for 5 to 8 hours, or until meat is very tender. Remove brisket from oven and peel back foil.

Raise oven temperature to 350°. Return brisket to oven and roast, uncovered, for 30 minutes to crisp the top layer of fat.

Allow meat to rest for 20 minutes. Slice across the grain into thin slices. Serve with Barbecue Sauce (see below).

Makes 10 to 12 servings.

For Brisket Sandwich: Serve sliced brisket on bun with barbecue sauce, onion, and pickle.

Texas is known for its long necks—specifically Lone Star Beer in the characteristic brown bottle with an elongated neck. Of course, there are other Texas brews with legions of fans: light beers like Pearl and Lone Star, dark beers like Shiner Bock. Almost as Texan are the array of Mexican beers. Some favorites include Carta Blanca, Bohemia, Tecate, and Corona.

And there's a whole new generation of craft beers made in Texas, with brews like St. Arnold's from Houston, leading the way. (See chapter 7.)

Brisket Sandwich, p. 133,
with Sauce, p. 134

Barbecue Sauce

1¼ cups ketchup
⅓ cup Worcestershire sauce
⅓ cup lemon juice
⅓ cup brown sugar
⅓ cup finely chopped onion
1 tablespoon yellow mustard
¼ cup water
1 clove garlic, crushed
¼ cup pan drippings from barbecue, optional

Combine ketchup, Worcestershire sauce, lemon juice, brown sugar, onion, mustard, water, and garlic in a medium saucepan. Place over very low heat and simmer, stirring occasionally, 1 hour.

Stir in pan drippings and cook 15 minutes longer.
Serve with sliced beef brisket.

It is easy to forget that a big chunk of Texas is beach, from Louisiana to Mexico. Seafood dishes like gumbo, especially near the Louisiana border, are an art form. Rice is the bed or crown for gumbo.

Gulf Gumbo

3 tablespoons vegetable oil
⅓ cup flour
1 cup chopped onion
½ cup green bell pepper, chopped
½ cup celery, chopped
2 cloves garlic, crushed
1 (28-ounce) can tomatoes, chopped (juice reserved)
6 cups chicken stock
½ cup bottled clam juice
1 (8-ounce) package frozen sliced okra
½ teaspoon leaf oregano
1 bay leaf
1 teaspoon black pepper
½ teaspoon cayenne pepper, or to taste
1 teaspoon salt, or to taste
1 pound seafood: peeled shrimp, crab, or whitefish (such as snapper or catfish), cut into 1-inch cubes (or a combination)
12 fresh oysters, liquid reserved, optional
1 tablespoon file powder
6 cups cooked rice

Tip: A lot of folks swear by rice cookers, but for me, a microwave is a built-in rice cooker. In a 2-quart microwave-safe dish with lid, combine 3 cups rice and 6 cups water. Add 2 teaspoons salt. Cook on high for 8 minutes or until liquid boils. Reduce power to medium and cook 25 minutes, or until rice is tender and liquid is absorbed. Fluff with a fork before serving. Makes 12 servings.

Heat vegetable oil in a large pot or dutch oven over low heat. Stir in flour and cook, stirring constantly, until flour is dark brown, about 30 minutes. Add onions, green pepper, celery, and garlic. Cook until vegetables soften and onions begin to brown.

Stir tomatoes and their juice, stock, and clam juice, into vegetables.

Add okra, oregano, bay leaf, black pepper, cayenne, and salt. Bring liquid to a boil; reduce heat and simmer, uncovered, about 30 minutes until vegetables are tender.

Gulf Gumbo, p. 135

Add seafood, except oysters, and cook just until seafood texture firms, about 5 minutes. Fish will turn white; shrimp will turn pink. If using, add oysters and their liquid during the last minute or so of cooking. Adjust seasoning to taste. Just before serving, add file (ground sassafras) to thicken gumbo to desired consistency. Do not allow liquid to boil again or file will appear stringy and clumpy and oysters will overcook.

Ladle gumbo over cooked rice in shallow bowls.

Makes 12 servings.

A "Mess O' Greens" is another holiday tradition for many Texans. Sometimes you'll find greens on a Thanksgiving or Christmas table. They're also wonderful with a spread, including ham, smoked turkey, or barbecue, on New Year's Day. Best of all these days, you can buy greens by the bag, already cleaned and torn into pieces for cooking.

A Big Pot o' Greens

3 bunches of turnip, collard, or mustard greens (or a
    combination) or 3 bags of ready-to-cook fresh greens
salt to taste
¼ pound salt pork or bacon, optional
3–4 dried small red peppers
1–2 cups chicken stock or water
1–2 tablespoons sugar, optional

Tear off thick stems and place greens in the sink. Cover with water. Sprinkle a small amount of salt over greens and stir. Allow water to settle a few minutes. Carefully lift out greens and place in a colander or large bowl. (If you have a double sink, the other side works great.)

Rinse out sink to eliminate any grit that may have dropped from greens. Return greens to sink and cover with water again. Allow any remaining grit to settle and unplug drain so that water runs out.

If using salt pork or bacon, cut into 1-inch pieces. Place in large pot over low heat and cook to melt the fat and lightly brown the pieces.

Tear large leaves into pieces and place in a large stockpot, dutch oven, or saucepan with a lid. Without shaking off too much water, add greens to pan, along with whole, dried red peppers.

If using ready-to-cook greens, add ½ cup liquid to the salt pork or bacon in the pan along with the greens.

It may be difficult to get all the greens in the pan, but cram them in. Cover pan with lid and place over medium heat. Cook just until leaves wilt and greens fit easily into pan.

Add enough additional water or chicken stock to almost cover greens. Bring liquid to a boil; reduce heat and simmer until greens are tender, about 20 minutes. Stir in sugar during last 10 minutes of cooking.

Makes 10 servings.

hili and Tamales (p. 179) are another flavor-intense combination for the day after. Chili is just as good served with a handful of crackers, tortilla chips, warm corn or flour tortillas, or corn bread (p. 18). Notice there are no beans in the chili recipe below. In Texas, beans are something you serve with chili as an option. Those that want beans with chili can add them. Chili is also great over rice with grated cheese and finely chopped onions.

Using canned enchilada sauce instead of tomato sauce gives the chili additional body as well as an extra wallop of heat. Don't be a wuss. Try it!

Chili con Carne

3 pounds coarsely ground beef or venison, or a mixture (divided use)
4 cloves garlic, crushed
7 tablespoons chili powder (divided use)
1 tablespoon ground cumin
1 (8-ounce) can tomato sauce or enchilada sauce
2 cups water, or as needed
3 tablespoons masa harina or instant dissolving flour
1 teaspoon salt, or to taste
1 teaspoon cayenne pepper, or to taste, optional
1 tablespoon paprika, optional

Place one-third of meat in a large saucepan or dutch oven over medium high heat. Cook until juices evaporate and meat begins to turn brown. Remove from pot and reserve. Repeat until all meat is cooked. Return meat to pot.

Lower heat and add garlic. Cook and stir until garlic softens and the fragrance is compelling. Stir in 6 tablespoons chili powder and cumin, mixing well to coat meat evenly. Add tomato or enchilada sauce and enough water to just barely cover meat.

Raise heat and bring liquid to a boil. Lower heat and simmer, covered, about 1 hour, or until meat is tender.

Chili con Carne, p. 138, and Corn Bread, p. 18, with Texas craft beer, p. 213

While stirring, sprinkle masa harina or flour over chili, 1 tablespoon at a time. Allow chili to cook and thicken between additions. Add masa or flour for desired consistency. Some cooks like soupy chili, others like theirs thick, like stew.

Cook, uncovered, for 20 minutes longer, or until liquid is slightly reduced and thickened. Add salt and cayenne pepper, if desired. Cayenne is quite spicy, so add according to taste.

Stir in paprika for a brighter red color. About 5 minutes before serving, stir in 1 tablespoon chili powder for a fresher chili flavor.

Makes 8 servings.

Pinto Beans

1 pound dry pinto beans
2 cups chopped onion
2 cloves garlic, crushed
½ cup ham or barbecue, cut in 1-inch chunks
4 cups water
1 fresh jalapeño, optional
1 teaspoon salt, or to taste
3 tablespoons chopped fresh cilantro, optional

Rinse beans in a colander. Place in a large saucepan or stock-pot with enough water to cover. Soak overnight or place over high heat and bring to a boil. Cook for 1 minute. Turn off heat, cover, and let beans soak for 1 hour.

When beans have finished soaking (either overnight or 1 hour in hot water), pour off soaking liquid. Rinse pot and return beans to pot. Add onions, garlic, meat, and water to cover by 1 inch. Add the jalapeño, if you want the heat.

Bring liquid to a boil over high heat. Lower temperature, cover, and simmer for 2 to 3 hours, or until beans are tender. When beans are tender, add salt to taste.

Just before serving, add cilantro, if desired.

Makes 10 servings.

VARIATION

* For refried beans, mash enough beans and small amount of their liquid to make 2 cups; reserve. (May use one 17-ounce can refried beans.) In a skillet over medium heat, cook ½ cup finely chopped onion in 1 tablespoon oil or bacon drippings until light brown, about 7 minutes. Add beans, stirring to mix well. Lower heat. Add some liquid from the beans if a softer consistency is desired. Add ½ teaspoon salt and ⅛ teaspoon pepper, or to taste.

Buzz's beans are too good to mix with chili. Eat 'em straight, ladled over corn bread. That's the way my late brother Buzz

Griffith enjoyed these beans after he cooked them for about six hours. They're also a wonderful side to barbecue or in a bowl over rice.

Buzz's Pot of Beans

1 pound pintos
½ pound black beans
½ pound red beans
3 onions, chopped, to make about 6 cups (divided use)
3 strips bacon, cut into 1-inch pieces
2 cubes chicken bouillon
2 teaspoons pepper
3 tablespoons chili powder
1 teaspoon cayenne pepper
1 whole head of garlic

Rinse beans and pick out any that are shriveled. Pour in a large bowl and add water to cover, at least 3 inches. Soak overnight. Pour off soaking liquid.

Place drained beans in a large stockpot or dutch oven. Add enough water to cover by 2 inches. Stir in 4 cups chopped onion, bacon, chicken bouillon cubes, pepper, chili powder, and cayenne.

Cut off the end of the garlic pod and pull off white paper-like layers. Leave unpeeled cloves attached to root end. Add to bean pot. Bring liquid to a boil over high heat. Lower heat and simmer, covered, for 2 to 3 hours, until beans are tender.

Add remaining 2 cups onion and cook 2 to 3 hours longer, covered. Add more liquid if necessary. Cook until beans are quite soft. Adjust seasoning to taste.

Makes 12 servings.

This is another hearty, flavorful soup to add to your list of bowl favorites. There are many versions of this soup. This one has a light stock as a base.

* Epazote is an herb that helps eliminate some of the gassiness of beans. It grows wild in much of Texas and Mexico and is becoming more available in supermarkets. It is easiest to find in Hispanic groceries. Add 1 tablespoon chopped fresh epazote, or 1 teaspoon dried, per pound of beans.

* For a thicker broth, use the back of a spoon to crush some of the cooked beans against the side of the pot. Stir the mashed beans into the broth. Repeat until desired thickness is achieved.

Tortilla Soup

½ cup vegetable oil (divided use)

1 cup chopped onion

2 cloves garlic, crushed

1 (8-ounce) can tomatoes with green chilies

4 cups chicken stock, canned, packaged or homemade (p. 240)

1 (8-ounce) can tomato or enchilada sauce

2 teaspoons chili powder (optional, or to taste if using enchilada sauce)

1 teaspoon ground cumin (optional, or to taste if using enchilada sauce)

1 teaspoon salt, or to taste

1 teaspoon pepper, or to taste

4 corn tortillas, cut into ½ × 1½-inch strips

1½ cups cooked chicken, cut in bite-size pieces

1 cup Monterey Jack cheese, grated

1 avocado, thinly sliced

½ cup sour cream

8 lime wedges

Heat 1 tablespoon vegetable oil in a large saucepan or dutch oven over medium heat. Add onions and garlic; cook until soft. Add tomatoes with green chilies, stock, and tomato sauce.

Stir in chili powder, cumin, salt, and pepper to taste. Reduce heat to low and simmer about 30 minutes.

Meanwhile, heat remaining oil in a small skillet over medium-high heat. Fry tortilla strips in batches until crisp. Drain on paper towels.

Add chicken and bring liquid to a boil. Remove from heat. Ladle soup into bowls and garnish each bowl with tortilla strips, a sprinkling of cheese, a few avocado slices, and a dollop of sour cream. Serve with a lime wedge.

Makes 8 servings.

Fried corn bread, called hush puppies, is a classic to serve with fried fish or other seafood. You can't make too many to go with a big pot of gumbo, either. But they're good with just about any soup, including chili.

Hush Puppies

2 cups yellow cornmeal
¼ cup flour
1 teaspoon baking soda
1 tablespoon baking powder
2 teaspoons salt
1 egg, lightly beaten
1½ cups buttermilk
⅓ cup finely chopped green onion, including some
    green part
vegetable or corn oil for frying

In a large bowl, stir together cornmeal, flour, baking soda, baking powder, and salt. Stir in egg, buttermilk, and onion, mixing just until ingredients are moistened.

Heat 2 inches of oil in a heavy skillet or wide saucepan to 375°. Drop batter by teaspoonfuls into hot oil and fry until golden brown on all sides, turning as necessary. Drain on paper towels.

Makes about 2 dozen.

My dad, Ed Griffith, called it Deer Hunter's Corn Bread or Hot Water Corn Bread, but it is basically fried cornmeal mush. It is most basic of cornmeal concoctions—cornmeal, water, and salt. If they were made "up North," they'd be called johnnycakes. They're also good with soups, gumbos, and chili. But I remember eating these as a kid on New Year's with a big bowl of Black-Eyed Peas (p. 193). Don't forget the sliced, fresh onion and jalapeños.

Hot Water Corn Bread

2 cups yellow cornmeal
1 teaspoon salt, or to taste
1 cup boiling water
oil for frying
¼ cup butter, at room temperature, optional

Combine cornmeal and salt in a large mixing bowl. Stir in hot water. Dough should be moist enough to hold a shape. Allow dough to cool enough to shape with your hands.

Spoon 1 heaping tablespoon of dough into the palm of one hand. Using both hands, shape the dough into a ½-inch-thick oval and place on wax paper.

Heat ½ inch oil in a skillet over medium-high heat. Slide corn bread patties into hot oil and cook until golden and crisp, 3 to 5 minutes. Turn and cook until golden, about 3 minutes longer. Drain on paper towels.

Keep warm. Brush with soft butter, if desired.

Makes 2 dozen.

This delicious salad is similar to a taco salad. Hearty and piquant, the queso dressing wilts the lettuce. It can be a meal in itself, with or without the addition of ground beef, shredded barbecue, or shredded chicken.

Queso Salad

1 (12-ounce) package salad blend (romaine lettuce preferred)
½ cup chopped green onion, including green part
1 avocado, peeled, pitted and cut into 1-inch pieces
1 cup tomato, cut into 1-inch pieces
½ cup Chile con Queso (see recipe p. 130) or use bottled queso
2 tablespoons chicken stock, or as needed
1 cup coarsely crushed tortilla chips

Toss together iceberg lettuce salad blend, green onion, avocado, and tomato.

Heat Chile con Queso. If needed, add chicken stock to thin to the consistency of a creamy salad dressing. Just before serving, pour warm cheese sauce over salad and toss to coat lettuce. Sprinkle with tortilla chips. Serve immediately.

Makes 6 servings.

VARIATIONS

* Crumble ½ pound ground beef into a large skillet over medium heat. Add ¼ teaspoon salt, ½ teaspoon ground cumin, and 1 garlic clove, crushed. Stir and cook until ground beef is well browned. Drain on absorbent paper towels to remove grease. Add to lettuce along with onion, avocado, and tomato.
* Or, instead of ground beef, add 1 cup shredded barbecue brisket or shredded chicken (grilled, roasted, or barbecued).

It only takes one spoonful of black-eyed peas anytime after midnight the first day of the New Year for prosperity and general good luck. A bite of peas can't hurt, so don't take any chances. Eat black-eyed peas on New Year's Eve and the first day of the New Year.

Black-eyed peas are usually served as a side dish. But a bowl full of black-eyed peas makes a great meal, plain, along with a wedge of Corn Bread (p. 18), or over rice. Of course, Lone Star Caviar (p. 155) also counts for luck on New Year's.

Black-Eyed Peas

1 (16-ounce) package frozen black-eyed peas with snaps
 or purple hull peas
1 cup chopped onion
1 cup water or chicken stock
2 strips bacon, cut into 1-inch pieces, optional
1 dried red japones chile or 1 fresh jalapeño, optional
1 teaspoon salt, or to taste
1 teaspoon pepper, or to taste

Combine black-eyed peas, onion, water or stock, bacon, and dried or fresh chile, if desired, in a medium saucepan over medium heat. Bring liquid to a boil; reduce heat to simmer. Cover saucepan and cook until peas are tender, about 30 to 45 minutes, depending on preferred texture.

Make sure too much liquid does not cook away. Black-eyed peas should be almost, but not quite, covered with liquid. When peas are tender, add salt and pepper to taste.

Makes 8 servings.

VARIATIONS

* For a Cajun touch, add 1½ tablespoons Old Bay (sea-food) seasoning and 2 teaspoons red pepper sauce during cooking. Just before serving, add 1½ cups cooked white rice seasoned with 1 teaspoon salt and 1 teaspoon pepper.
* For a Tex-Mex touch, add 1 (10-ounce) can diced tomatoes with green chilies, 2 tablespoons fresh lime juice, and about 6 tablespoons chopped fresh cilantro leaves just before serving.

I have people over for New Year's Day just about every year. The menu varies from year to year, but the peas are always there. It is surprising how many people are still ready to party "the day after." People come and go with no set time for arrival or leaving. It's a good way to celebrate because, at last, "the holidays are over."

—*Prissy Shaffer*

New Year's Day is rightfully noted as a day of recovery as well as optimism. Red chile posole has become a tradition among my friends in Marfa where we gather to celebrate the New Year.

This recipe may be made with hominy or with fresh posole, corn that has been soaked in lye water. The term for this in Spanish is *nixtamal*. This is the same process used to make hominy for grits. It makes corn easier to digest and removes the hull.

Red Chile Posole

2 pounds pork shoulder, cut into 1-inch cubes
large onion, finely chopped
3 to 4 cloves garlic, minced
1 (32-ounce) package frozen fresh posole or 4 cups drained and rinsed white or yellow hominy
2 (14-ounce) container frozen red chile, thawed
3 bay leaves
3 to 4 cups chicken stock, or as needed
traditional garnishes: dried Mexican oregano; finely minced serrano or jalapeño pepper; finely minced white or yellow onion; minced fresh cilantro

Trim a few pieces of fat from pork and place in bottom of large, deep pot or dutch oven over medium to medium-high heat. Add ⅓ of the pork and brown pieces evenly. Remove from pan and reserve. Repeat with remaining pork until all pieces are browned.

Add onions to pot and cook until edges are golden and onion is soft, 3 to 5 minutes. Add garlic and cook another minute or so.

Return pork to pan. Add posole or hominy. Stir in thawed red chile sauce and bay leaves. Add enough chicken stock to cover the meat. Bring liquid to a boil. Lower heat and simmer 1 to 2 hours or until pork is tender.

If time allows, refrigerate posole overnight. Lift off any solidified fat before reheating.

Serve in large bowls with traditional garnishes, which can be added according to individual taste.

Makes 8 to 10 servings.

Food Gifts
for Thanksgiving through New Year's Day

There's certainly no shortage of fabulous gourmet food gifts for sale in stores, catalogs, online, and just about any retail venue. No matter how many unique and wonderful products are available, something homemade, whether alone or combined with luxury products, is the most heartfelt.

Whether the meaning is "hello," "thanks," or "happy holidays," this assortment will provide at least one perfect medium for your message. Of course, the best Texas food gift not only tastes good but says "Texas" in style and ingredients.

This chapter is devoted to gift recipes and ideas. However, each of the other chapters has recipes that can also serve as gifts. The list on the next page will whet your appetite and imagination. And remember, you really can't be too Texan when it comes to making and packaging Texas food gifts. There's never a better time to flaunt your Texas pride.

How to Make a Texas Gift Basket

Assembling a gift basket with homemade goodies, gourmet products, or a combination is one of the most personal expressions of gifting. Unique gift baskets can often be just the solution when you can't decide what to give. You can use different shapes of baskets, with or without a handle, and the size depends on what you want to put into it. Pack your gift container compactly if you plan to mail it. Ask the mail center to box it to make sure nothing inside will break.

TIPS:

* Wrap baskets in cellophane: clear or colored, print or festive. Use about 1½ to 2 yards, depending on size of basket.
* Ready-made bows take the hassle out of making one, but make sure that the size is right for the basket—a large basket requires a larger bow. Likewise, don't hide a small basket with an oversized bow. Also consider using raffia, ribbon, thin rope, or tinsel. You'll need 2 to

3 yards. Gather the cellophane with a twist tie or rubber band. Then secure the bow and/or ribbon, etc.

* Other containers can be used instead of a basket, such as a casserole dish, pie plate, serving bowl, or gift box bottom. Let your imagination go wild.
* The gift tag can be attached by a string from the gathered bow, or taped to the front of the basket. Don't forget to include instructions for using the gift such as a recipe idea card.

This fudge is so simple you'll want to make several batches for gifting as well as for having on hand. No Texas Christmas is complete without fudge and Divinity (see p. 110). Decorated with crushed peppermint, this will make you a holiday legend.

Chocolate Peppermint Fudge

2½ cups sugar
½ cup unsalted butter
¼ teaspoon salt
1 (5-ounce) can evaporated milk (not sweetened condensed milk), about ⅔ cup
1 (7-ounce) jar marshmallow creme, about 2 cups
1 (12-ounce) package semisweet chocolate chips, about 2 cups
¾ cup finely chopped pecans
1 teaspoon vanilla
2 to 3 drops peppermint extract, optional
1½ cups peppermint candy

Line a 9-inch square pan with foil so that foil extends over the sides of the pan. Rub foil with butter.

Combine sugar, butter, salt, and evaporated milk in a 2-quart microwave-safe bowl. A large glass measuring bowl with a handle works particularly well. Microwave on high for 6 to 8 minutes, or until mixture comes to a rolling boil, stirring twice.

Add marshmallow creme and chocolate chips; blend until smooth. Stir in pecans, vanilla, and peppermint extract,

Chocolate Peppermint Fudge, p. 150

if desired. Pour into buttered, foil-lined pan. Allow to cool slightly. Meanwhile, process peppermint in food processor to crush. Sprinkle crushed peppermint evenly over top of fudge.

Cool to room temperature. Using the tip of a knife, mark the fudge into 36 squares. Refrigerate until firm.

To remove fudge from pan, lift foil from pan. Remove foil from sides of fudge. Cut through the lines to make 36 pieces. Store fudge in refrigerator.

VARIATION

* For White Chocolate Fudge, substitute white chocolate chips for semisweet chocolate chips. Proceed as above. Makes 36 pieces.

Pecans have a way of showing up in all sorts of recipes, from the beginning to the end of the meal. They're quite simply Texans' favorite nuts. They grow wonderfully well, particularly in the heart of the state. In exchange, Texans have taken them to heart.

Here are sweet and savory versions.

Sugared Pecans

2 cups sugar
1 teaspoon cinnamon
¼ teaspoon cream of tartar
½ cup boiling water
4 cups (1 pound) pecan halves
1 teaspoon vanilla

Combine sugar, cinnamon, cream of tartar, and boiling water in a small saucepan over medium heat. Stirring constantly, cook until boiling and boil until candy thermometer reaches 240° (soft-ball stage).

Remove from heat and stir in pecans. Allow to cool a few minutes. Add vanilla and stir until pecans are coated. Pour pecans onto waxed paper and separate.

Makes 4 cups.

Spicy Pecans

4 cups (1 pound) pecan halves
4 tablespoons butter
1–2 tablespoons Worcestershire sauce, or to taste
1 teaspoon lemon juice
¼ teaspoon cayenne pepper or to taste
2 teaspoons salt, or to taste

Preheat oven to 200°. Place pecans on a jelly roll pan. Melt butter in a small saucepan over low heat. Remove from heat and add Worcestershire sauce, lemon juice, and cayenne pepper. Mix well and pour over pecans, stirring to coat all sides, and arrange in single layer in pan.

Spicy Pecans, p. 152, and Sugared Pecans, p. 152

Place in oven and bake for 45 to 60 minutes or until pecans become toasty and brown. Stir occasionally while cooking. Remove from oven and sprinkle with salt to taste, stirring to coat all sides.

Cool completely and store in airtight container for giving. For storage longer than a couple of weeks, place in freezer containers and freeze.

Makes about 4 cups.

VARIATION

* For Salted Pecans, omit cayenne pepper.

Nothing says Texas like chili. A jar, tin, or packet of your personal chili powder blend is a great way to send a taste of the Lone Star State to someone far from home. To truly customize this chili blend, experiment with some of your favorite spices in whatever proportions you prefer. Make a gift basket with chili powder, a recipe card for chili . . . and include some of your new secret ingredient for really piquant chile: enchilada sauce (see recipe, p. 138).

Custom-Blend Chili Powder

6 ounces (about ¾ cup) ground ancho chilies or other dried ground red chili
1 tablespoon ground cumin
1 tablespoon garlic powder
1–2 teaspoons cayenne pepper, or to taste
2 teaspoons powdered oregano
2 tablespoons paprika

Combine ground red chilies, cumin, garlic, cayenne pepper, oregano, and paprika. Shake to blend well. Three tablespoons will season 2 pounds of ground beef or coarsely ground beef or venison.

Makes about 1 cup.

Give the gift of Custom-Blend Chili Powder along with a pot of chili made with it—and a copy of the recipe on a recipe card. Put "Your Name" on it so the giftee will remember who to thank for the best bowl of red ever.

"Your Name's" Favorite Chili

2 pounds ground beef or coarsely ground beef or venison for chili
3 tablespoons chili blend
1 (8-ounce) can enchilada sauce
2–3 cups water, or as needed
1–2 tablespoons masa harina or instant dissolving flour

Tip: When giving food gifts, include storage and preparation instructions. Foods that require refrigeration should say so on the label. Also, remember to date the container as well. A copy of the recipe is often appreciated, too.

Place ground meat in dutch oven or large saucepan over medium heat. Cook until meat is no longer pink and liquid has evaporated. Do not brown too much.

Mix in chili blend and stir to coat meat evenly. Add enchilada sauce and just enough water to cover meat. Bring liquid to a boil, reduce heat, and simmer, covered, until meat is tender, about 1 to 1½ hours.

Dissolve masa or flour in 2 tablespoons water to make a smooth paste. Stir into chili until broth thickens and no lumps remain. Allow to simmer until desired consistency is reached, about 20 minutes. Adjust seasoning to taste.

Makes 4 to 6 servings.

This relish is wonderful as a condiment or dip. It also counts as good luck on New Year's Day.

Lone Star Caviar (Black-Eyed Pea Relish)

1 (16-ounce) package frozen black-eyed peas
1 cup green bell pepper, chopped into pieces about the size of black-eyed peas
1 cup red bell pepper, chopped into pieces about the size of black-eyed peas
¼ cup finely chopped jalapeño pepper, ribs and seeds removed
1 cup yellow onion, chopped into pieces about the size of black-eyed peas
1 cup finely chopped green onion, including green tops
2 cloves garlic, finely chopped
1 cup finely chopped parsley
¾ cup vegetable or olive oil
¼ cup lime or lemon juice
1 teaspoon maple syrup, optional
2 teaspoons salt, or to taste
1 teaspoon pepper, or to taste

Tip: Serving suggestions for Lone Star Caviar as:

* Relish with barbecue, roasted, or grilled meats
* Bean salad
* Garnish for tomato slices or green beans
* Dip for chips or vegetable crudités
* "Top-enade" for East Texas "Polenta," p. 124

Cook black-eyed peas, according to package instructions, or just until tender, 15 to 20 minutes. Drain well.

Lone Star Caviar, p. 155

Place black-eyed peas in a large mixing bowl. Toss with peppers, onions, garlic, and parsley. Whisk together oil, lime or lemon juice, maple syrup, salt, and pepper. Adjust seasoning to taste. Pour over vegetables and refrigerate overnight to meld flavors.

Place in refrigerator containers for giving. Store up to 1 week, refrigerated.

Makes 6 cups.

⟡

This used to be a Texas curiosity, but piquant, excellent jelly for roast or grilled meats, especially pork or game, has spread way beyond our borders. The tried-and-true presentation, however, is to spoon the jelly over a log of cream cheese as a spread for crackers.

Jalapeño Jelly

1 cup chopped green bell peppers, seeded, ribs and stems
   removed
⅓ cup chopped fresh jalapeño peppers, seeded, ribs and
   stems removed (wear rubber gloves when handling hot
   peppers and avoid contact with eyes, nose, or lips)
1½ cups apple cider vinegar
6 cups sugar
1 (6-ounce) bottle pectin
green food color, optional

Combine bell peppers and jalapeños in work bowl of a food
processor. Add vinegar and process until peppers are a
smooth puree.

Place in saucepan with sugar over medium-high heat.
Bring to a rolling boil and boil for 5 minutes. Remove from
heat and pour in pectin. Add color, if desired, to achieve bright,
green color. Stir for 2 to 3 minutes. Pour into sterilized jelly jars
to within ¼ inch of the rim and seal with manufacturer's lids.
Store in refrigerator up to 6 months. Process according to can-
ning instructions for shelf storage.

Makes 8 (½-pint) jars.

Chile petin jelly is hot stuff. The green Jalapeño Jelly pales
in comparison because of the heat created by the tiny red
chilies called *petins* or *tepins*, depending on who you ask. Small
and round, these peppers are available dried year-round. If you
can't find them, substitute *pequins*. Susan Hamilton Smith of
San Antonio grows her own and makes the jelly from fresh peppers that turn from green to red at the end of summer when the
days are as hot as the chilies. Handle these carefully, especially
fresh ones. The juices can burn fingers, eyes, lips, and noses.
Wear gloves, and don't get too close to the fumes.

Chile Petin Jelly

¼ cup fresh red chile petins (or ⅛ cup dried)
¾ cup yellow bell pepper
6½ cups sugar
1½ cups apple cider vinegar
6 ounces liquid fruit pectin

If using fresh chilies, handle carefully. Remove stems from fresh or dried. Remove seeds and ribs from bell pepper. Chop coarsely to make ¾ cup.

Place chilies and bell pepper in the work bowl of a food processor. Pulse on and off to chop fine.

Place chopped chilies in a large saucepan with sugar and cider vinegar. Bring to a boil over high heat and boil for 2 minutes. Remove from heat and allow to cool 5 minutes. Add fruit pectin. Return to high heat and boil for 1 minute.

Pour into 7 (8-ounce) hot sterile jars. Seal and store in refrigerator, up to 6 months.

Makes 7 (8-ounce) jars.

No holiday season is complete without encountering a batch of retro-chic cereal mix, or Texas Trash, as it is often called. Go heavy on the pecans, and you'll have it Texas-style.

Texas Trash

1 (15-ounce) package round oat cereal
1 (12-ounce) package crispy waffle rice cereal
1 (12-ounce) package crispy waffle corn cereal
1 (9-ounce) package pretzel sticks
2 cups pecan halves
1 cup cashews
2 cups peanuts
2 cups (4 sticks) butter
½–¾ cup Worcestershire sauce, or to taste
3 teaspoons garlic salt, or to taste
1–2 teaspoons red pepper sauce, optional

In large bowl, toss together cereals, pretzels, and nuts.

Heat oven to 325°. Place butter in a large roasting pan with sides. Melt butter in oven. When butter melts, remove pan from oven and stir in Worcestershire sauce, garlic salt, and red pepper sauce, if desired.

Stir cereal mixture into melted butter, tossing to coat each piece. Place in oven and bake for 30 to 40 minutes, or until cereal is golden brown and crisp.

Store in airtight container up to 30 days.

Makes 3 to 3½ quarts.

———

Fresh salsas are means of self-expression. You can go traditional with pico de gallo or contemporary with variations that incorporate fruit and other vegetables. Use this basic recipe with variations as inspiration to add your own touches.

Chips and Salsa, p. 161

Pico de Gallo (Fresh Tomato Salsa)

4 large, ripe tomatoes (about 2 cups coarsely chopped)
2–3 tablespoons finely chopped fresh jalapeño peppers, or
  to taste
½ cup onion, coarsely chopped
2 cloves garlic, finely chopped
juice from ½ to 1 lime, or to taste
1 teaspoon salt, or to taste
3 tablespoons fresh cilantro, finely chopped

Combine tomatoes, peppers, onion, garlic, and lime juice in a medium bowl. Toss to combine. Add salt, mixing well. Adjust seasoning to taste. Allow to stand about 1 hour. Add cilantro, mixing well. Transfer to container with tight-fitting lid. Store in refrigerator up to 1 week.

Makes 2½ cups.

VARY BY SUBSTITUTING:

* Coarsely chopped pineapple for tomatoes; add 2 tablespoons minced red bell pepper or use red jalapeño
* 1 cup chopped peeled cucumber and 1 cup chopped honeydew melon for tomatoes
* Chopped mango for tomatoes; add 2 tablespoons minced red bell pepper or use red jalapeño

After dinner, for several nights before Christmas, Mama would clear the table, make lots of hot chocolate, and put out all the package wrappings: glistening colored ribbons, rolls of wrapping paper, and all kinds of decorations, including my favorite—glitter in every color imaginable to affix with invisible glue. First, the edges of the paper had to be folded just right and the scotch tape couldn't show. I loved this time with my mom and getting to help design the packages for everyone in the family. Daddy and my brother, Bill, "coached" by nodding approval as they watched television and had seconds of pecan pie.

—Dedie Leahy

This is a basic cooked salsa which may also be tuned up to suit your taste and personality. It may be canned for shelf storage or put in airtight containers for refrigerated storage.

Salsa

- 1 (28-ounce) can Italian tomatoes, with juice
- 1 cup onion, finely chopped
- 1 teaspoon fresh serrano pepper, seeded and finely chopped
- 2 tablespoons fresh jalapeño pepper, seeded and finely chopped
- 3 cloves garlic, finely chopped
- ½ teaspoon salt, or to taste
- 1 teaspoon sugar, or to taste

Place tomatoes in food processor and pulse on and off to finely chop. Add onion, peppers, garlic, salt, and sugar. Pulse 2 to 3 times to blend and achieve desired consistency. Do not puree mixture, but leave small chunks of tomatoes and peppers visible.

Pour into a medium saucepan and place over medium heat. Bring to a boil; lower heat and simmer for 30 minutes, or until slightly thickened. Cool slightly and pour into ½-pint jars. Refrigerate up to 3 to 4 weeks.

Makes 4 (½-pint) jars.

Peanut brittle is a long-standing holiday tradition. Making it in the microwave is the easiest trick of all. If you want to spice this up, add a touch of cayenne for a sweet-hot treat. This doesn't make a huge batch. It's easier to make multiple batches than to expand the recipe.

Peanut Brittle

1 cup raw peanuts, shells and skins removed
½ cup white corn syrup
1 cup sugar
⅛ teaspoon salt
¼ teaspoon cayenne pepper or *esplette* (smoked pimento powder), optional
1 teaspoon butter
1 teaspoon vanilla
1 teaspoon baking soda

Generously butter a cookie sheet. Set aside.

Combine peanuts, corn syrup, sugar, salt, and cayenne in a 1½- to 2-quart glass measuring dish, preferably one with a handle, like a big measuring cup. Microwave on high for 8 minutes, stirring with a wooden spoon every 2 minutes.

Add butter and vanilla. Microwave on high 2 minutes longer, without stirring. Add baking soda and stir. Working quickly, pour candy mixture onto buttered cookie sheet, in an even layer, distributing peanuts as evenly as possible. Cool completely.

Break into 2- to 3-inch pieces and store in an airtight container.

Makes 15 to 20 pieces.

Lavender thrives in part of Texas as in southern France; fields of lilac bloom in the Texas Hill Country. Chocolate, lavender, bourbon: lovely flavors and fragrances. And very Texas! Give a box of these for the holidays.

Texas Chocolate Bourbon Balls with Lavender

1 (14-ounce) can sweetened condensed milk
3 cups bittersweet chocolate chips
1 tablespoon vanilla extract
2 tablespoons bourbon
½ teaspoon dried lavender
confectioners' sugar and unsweetened cocoa

Combine sweetened condensed milk and chocolate chips in a saucepan over low heat. Heat, stirring, until melted and smooth; remove from heat. Stir in the vanilla, bourbon, and lavender. Transfer to a small bowl. Cover and chill for 3 to 4 hours, or until mixture is firm.

When firm enough to hold a shape, shape mixture into 1-inch balls; roll in confectioners' sugar or cocoa. Place on a tray or baking sheet, cover loosely, and chill for at least 1 hour. For gifting or buffet service, place each truffle in a foil cup.

Store in tightly covered container in the refrigerator until giving or serving.

Makes 32 truffles.

These traditional Southern goodies are wonderful with Spicy Pecans or with any selection of hors d'oeuvres. This version is an adaption of food stylist Martha Gooding's mother's recipe. They're also memorable with a simple soup.

Cheese Straws

1 cup unsalted butter, at room temperature
2½ cups flour
½ teaspoon salt
¼ to ½ teaspoon cayenne pepper
2 cups grated sharp cheddar cheese

Preheat oven to 350°. In food processor, combine butter, flour, salt, and cayenne, pulsing to combine. Add cheese and pulse a few times to combine. Refrigerate 30 minutes to 1 hour for easier handling.

Using about ⅓ of dough, roll thin, about ¼ inch thick. Cut into thin strips, about ½ inch wide and 2 inches long, or load dough into a cookie press and extrude thin strips, about 2 inches long. Place strips on cookie sheet.

Bake for 10 to 15 minutes, or just until golden. Allow cookie sheet to cool between batches. Repeat until all dough is used.

Makes about 5 dozen.

Yet another traditional food gift in Texas is a loaf of pumpkin, or any other quick bread.

Pumpkin Bread

3⅓ cups flour
2 teaspoons baking soda
1 teaspoon nutmeg
3 teaspoons cinnamon
1 teaspoon salt
3 cups sugar
1 cup vegetable oil
⅔ cup water
4 eggs, well beaten
1 (16-ounce) can pumpkin
1 teaspoon vanilla
1 cup coarsely chopped pecans
1 cup raisins

Preheat oven to 350°. Grease 3 (8- or 9-inch) loaf pans. For individual gifts, grease 6 to 8 mini-loaf pans.

Sift together flour, baking soda, nutmeg, cinnamon, and salt. In a large bowl, combine sugar, oil, and water. Stir in dry ingredients.

Add eggs, pumpkin, and vanilla, mixing to combine. Do not overbeat. Fold in pecans and raisins. Pour batter into prepared pans. Bake for 55 to 60 minutes, or until toothpick inserted in center comes out clean. Bake mini-loaf pans about 40 minutes, or until loaf tests done.

Makes 3 (8- or 9-inch) loaf pans or 6 to 8 mini-loaf pans.

This is an incredibly rich cake. Rum is a very traditional holiday flavoring. So is bourbon. Take your pick. Using a Texas-made spirit makes this gift even more spectacular. Giving the bottle along with the cake is a very major gift. No chance that will be regifted.

Put this in a basket along with the Bundt pan and/or a carton of eggnog. Better yet, make your own Eggnog now, p. 118.

If gifting this cake, omit the optional topping. Suggest serving with whipped cream or ice cream. If making this cake as a gift to yourself for serving right away, you may want to add the optional topping.

Rum (Bourbon) Cake

4 cups all-purpose flour
½ teaspoon baking powder
4 sticks (1 pound) butter, softened at room temperature
2⅔ cups sugar
10 eggs
1 teaspoon vanilla
1 tablespoon dark rum (or bourbon)
sifted confectioners' sugar, as desired
whipped cream, as desired
optional topping (see below)

Preheat oven to 350°. Grease and flour a 10-inch Bundt or tube pan. Sift together flour and baking powder into a small bowl.

In the bowl of an electric mixer, beat together at high speed the softened butter and sugar until light and fluffy. Mix in eggs, one at a time, beating well after each addition. Blend in vanilla and rum or bourbon.

Gradually add the dry ingredients and beat on medium speed for 2 minutes. Pour batter into prepared pan. Before placing in oven, carefully lift pan an inch or so and drop back to counter. Do this several times to release air bubbles. Level top of cake with spatula. Bake for 55 minutes or until cake tests done.

Remove cake from oven and let cool for about 5 minutes. Run a knife along edges of pan, if necessary, to free the cake from the sides. Turn out onto a wire rack to cool.

Just before serving, dust with sifted confectioners' sugar and top each serving with whipped cream. Or add optional topping (see below).

Makes 12 to 16 servings.

Optional glaze topping: Melt 1 stick butter (½ cup) in small saucepan. Add 1 cup sugar and ¼ cup water. Bring to a boil over high heat. When mixture boils, remove from heat and add 1 tablespoon rum or bourbon or to taste. When cake is done, remove from oven and leave in pan. Gently prick holes into the cake with a skewer. Slowly, so glaze topping can soak in, pour half the topping over bottom of cake. If desired, add ½ finely chopped pecans to glaze topping. Let cake cool for about 5 minutes. Run a knife along edges of pan, if necessary, to free the cake from the sides. Turn out onto cake plate or platter. If using, spoon pecans evenly around top of cake. Pour remaining topping over top of cake. Cool completely.

Thanksgiving, Christmas, or on a Thursday at our house on Hilltop Road in Fort Worth, it was always the perfect time for Mama's Pecan Pie. My lovely, savvy mother, Elizabeth Honnet Leahy, was creative and meticulous in the kitchen. This recipe was handed down from her mother, my grandmother, Delia, after whom I am named. This pie became famous because everyone loves it and no one can figure it out! So, it's quite a special recipe, which will be a hit with everyone, especially the men—it's an all-time favorite of all the men in the Leahy family. Recently, I added dark chocolate because my husband, Rick Turner, loves it, and why not?! Now, it's a favorite of the Turner clan as well.

—Dedie Leahy

This is an amazing pie that you've got to try. Make one for yourself and give the other as a gift. They're easy enough to make multiples. The egg white batter forms a meringue topping that is light and delicious. With its cracked surface, this is a lovely pie for eating or gifting.

Dedie's Cracked Chocolate Pecan Pie

11 whole graham crackers, finely ground (generous ¾ cup)
1 teaspoon baking powder
1 cup chopped pecans
3 egg whites
1 cup sugar
1 teaspoon vanilla
1 cup semisweet chocolate chunks or chips

Preheat oven to 350°. Grease a 9- or 10-inch ovenproof glass pie plate.

Process graham crackers in food processor until finely ground. Or place crackers between two sheets of wax paper and crush with rolling pin. In large bowl, stir together graham cracker crumbs, baking powder, and chopped pecans; reserve.

In a second large bowl, beat egg whites at high speed until frothy and beginning to turn white. Beating constantly, gradually add sugar and vanilla; beat until egg whites are stiff. To test, remove beaters and turn upside down. if peaks remain upright, egg whites are "beaten stiff."

Fold crumb mixture into egg whites. Using a large rubber spatula, gradually add crumb mixture. To fold in ingredients, move the whites only as much as necessary so as not to deflate them. Hold the spatula with the flat side of the spatula facing toward you. Grip edge of bowl with other hand. Bring the spatula straight down into the whites, cutting through the center of the mixture. Repeat, turning bowl slightly, until all crumbs are "folded in."

Fold in the chocolate chunks, using same technique. Turn mixture into prepared pie plate. Bake for 25 to 30 minutes until golden on top.

Makes 8 servings.

The Ultimate Holiday Gift

This technique came to me courtesy of my friends Elaine Corn and Peggy Kligman when I came down with a bad cold when we were in Marfa for New Year's Eve. Thus it is a true gift of love and caring.

This rich stock, a.k.a. Jewish penicillin, is magic for stuffy noses and achy bodies. Elaine credits her Chinese husband, Chef David Soohoo, for teaching her how to make this loving stock pot of steaming hot healing. Take a pot of this to a friend suffering from a cold during the holidays; that's the spirit of the season.

It's also a wonderful rich stock for soups or any use calling for chicken stock. I've added seasoning alternatives: Asian (with ginger and garlic) and European (celery, onion, and carrot).

Either way, this technique produces an extraordinarily rich, clear stock. Bonus: the chicken is plump and moist, even when shredded, instead of being stringy and spent as boiled chicken too often is.

Chewish Chicken Chtock

1 whole fryer
4 to 5 quarts water or as needed
1 knuckle of ginger plus 4 cloves garlic plus 1 tablespoon whole black peppercorns
or
2 ribs celery plus 1 onion plus 1 large carrot plus 1 tablespoon whole black peppercorns
salt to taste

Remove giblets and neck from cavity of chicken. Discard liver or use for chopped chicken liver. Place chicken into large stew pot and add enough water to cover the bird. Toss gizzard and chicken neck into pot.

Place stew pot on cold burner, uncovered. Turn heat to medium high. As the pot heats, skim the foam from the edges of the pot.

This may take up to an hour, depending on size of chicken and amount of liquid. Be patient. Don't let the liquid come to a boil. Liquid should simmer ever so gently, just so the bubbles occasionally break the surface. Adjust heat as needed so liquid stays at a gentle simmer. Continue to skim foam as needed. Cook this way for an hour after liquid bubbles. Do not cover. After 30 to 40 minutes of low simmer, turn chicken to fully immerse breast.

After chicken has simmered for about an hour, place lid on pot, turn off heat, and steep for 30 minutes. Carefully remove chicken from stock and place in a large bowl to catch any drippings; allow to cool enough to handle. Add ginger, garlic, and peppercorns; or, celery, onion, and carrot (each cut into several pieces) and peppercorns, depending on whether Asian or European flavor profile is desired. Optional additions to European profile: 3 bay leaves and a small bundle of parsley.

Pull chicken meat from bones and allow meat to cool completely. Place bones in stock. Return stock to medium to low heat, add drippings, and gently simmer, uncovered, until liquid is reduced by nearly half, about an hour. Season to taste with salt. Skim occasionally as needed.

Cool liquid and strain to remove bones and vegetables; discard the solids. Refrigerate stock several hours or overnight so fat rises to the top and congeals. Scrape off and discard solid fat. Reserve congealed stock for use in any recipe calling for chicken stock; or sip, steaming hot, to relieve upper respiratory congestion.

Meanwhile, remove and discard skin from chicken meat. Cut chicken meat into bite-size pieces for use in another dish or in chicken soup. To shred the breast meat, pull small pieces in strings, going with the grain to produce shreds.

Makes 3 to 4 quarts stock plus meat from chicken.

From top, left to right:
Row 1: Chef Hoover Alexander,
Chef Monica Pope, Chef Dean
Fearing, Chef Stephan Pyles
Row 2: Chef Tim Perini,
Estella Martinez and
Chef Matt Martinez Jr.
Row 3: Chef Johnny Hernandez,
Chef Sylvia Casares,
Chef Tim Love
Row 4: Chef Jeff Blank,
Chef Robert Del Grande,
Chef Grady Spears

Texas Chefs' Holiday Favorites

The state of Texas cuisine just keeps getting better through the work and vision of Lone Star chefs who shine so brightly. Some, such as Stephan Pyles, who wrote the foreword for the first edition of this book and kindly agreed to update his message for this one, Dean Fearing, Robert Del Grande, and Jeff Blank, were in the first wave of chefs that put Texas on the culinary map.

Others have come on the scene in ensuing years. Monica Pope was among the leaders of the farm-to-table movement. Johnny Hernandez brings Mexican street food to life in Texas. Sylvia Casares' food and memories embrace the unique culture of South Texas. Matt Martinez Jr.'s beloved Tex-Mex traditions are maintained by his wife, Estella, and their family. Hoover Alexander's distinctive African American and Southern touches round out the Texas experience. Cowboy chefs Tom Perini, Tim Love, and Grady Spears embody the myth with their down-to-earth haute cuisine.

Each generously contributed a recipe and a holiday memory. Thank you, my friends, and happy holidays, always.

Dotty Griffith

Hoover Alexander

HOOVER'S COOKING,
HOOVER'S SOULAR FOOD TRAILER & GARDEN

Austin

Hoover Alexander opened his barbecue and soul food restaurant in East Austin in 1998. Since then he's become a fixture in his community and recently spearheaded a community garden, food truck, and culinary classroom called Soular Food Trailer & Garden.

Alexander began his 30-plus-year culinary career at the legendary Night Hawk restaurant in Austin. He's fifth-generation Texan and knows how Texans like to celebrate when it comes to food.

Besides barbecue, he's known for his fruit cobblers, meat loaf, collards, catfish, and chicken-fried steak. Hoover's a force on the Austin culinary scene.

Hoover Alexander's Mom's Tomato Preserves

18 medium-size tomatoes
3½ cups plus ¼ cup sugar (divided use)
2 tablespoons plus 3 teaspoons lemon juice (divided use)
3 ounces Sure-Jell gelatin
¼ teaspoon salt
¼ teaspoon ground cloves

Drop tomatoes, one by one, into a large pot of boiling water. After all tomatoes have been submerged in water for 2 to

3 minutes, cut off heat. Remove tomatoes from water and cool enough to handle. Peel and remove core. Using a food processor, chop coarsely.

Place tomatoes and their juices into a large, heavy-bottom saucepan. Add 3½ cups sugar and 2 tablespoons lemon juice. Bring liquid to a boil; reduce heat and simmer for 1 hour.

Add remaining ¼ cup sugar, 3 teaspoons lemon juice, gelatin, salt, and cloves. Cook over low heat for 1 hour.

Meanwhile, place 8 half-pint jars into boiling water for 5 minutes. Drain. When tomatoes are cooked, spoon preserves into jars, seal, and place on rack in pan of boiling water for 5 minutes. Remove to a rack and cool.

Makes 8 jars.

Jeff Blank

HUDSON'S ON THE BEND, MIGHTY CONE

Austin

Jeff opened the restaurant that has become a Hill Country legend in 1984 in an area near Lake Travis, one of the six Highland Lakes in the scenic Texas Hill Country west of Austin. The name "Hudson's on the Bend" is a nod to the area nearby known as Hudson Bend where a family named Hudson settled on a bend in the Colorado River. This native Texan's casual country place specializes in wild game: venison, wild boar, pheasant, and quail. Jeff has been a fearless chef and priceless character his entire career.

In addition to his famed menu, cooking classes, cookbooks, and gourmet sauce line, Jeff has become a major player in the Austin food truck universe with his Mighty Cone trailer.

Jeff and longtime restaurant manager and friend Sara Courington keep Hudson's on the Bend as authentic as ever, right down to the herb garden that flanks the walkway.

Holidays always meant great food for our family. My mother was famous for her yeast rolls. She'd only make those on the holidays and it was a labor of love. She'd make plenty of extra. People would drop by and want to pick up a few extra . . . six dozen or so. She'd cook for days and days. She's just programmed to do it, staying up until the wee hours. Then she'd be in bed and sick for two days after Christmas. As she's gotten older, she's doing less of that. One thing I always love with those yeast rolls is something that brings back memories of the family farm right outside of Austin: when there was a bounty of tomatoes, she'd can and put things up. I can't get enough of her tomato preserves. I still love putting those on biscuits or yeast rolls.

—Hoover Alexander

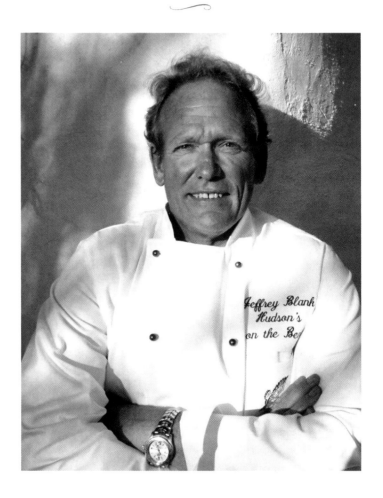

Hill Country Holiday Eggs with Smoked Wild Pig, Basil Lime-daise, and Potato Pancakes

POTATO PANCAKES

4 medium russet potatoes, unpeeled and scrubbed well
1½ cups smoked bacon, fried, drained, and finely chopped
4 garlic cloves, finely chopped
1 cup red onions, finely chopped
¼ cup flour
3 whole eggs
2 teaspoons salt, or to taste . . . potatoes really suck up the salt
½ teaspoon cayenne pepper
¼ cup vegetable oil, more if needed

Grate potatoes in food processor using coarse grating blade or grate by hand. Drain. Combine potatoes and remaining ingredients except the vegetable oil in a bowl, blending well. Hands work best. Squeeze out the liquid and shape into English muffin–size pancakes.

In a large skillet, heat the vegetable oil and sauté potato pancakes over medium heat until golden brown and crunchy, about 10 minutes. Allow 2 potato pancakes per serving.

Reserve on a paper towel–lined baking sheet.

Makes at least 20 pancakes.

The pancakes are truly sturdy and can be done hours before final assembly. Jeff's "unbreakable Hollandaise" can be prepared 3 to 4 hours ahead of time and held in a thermal pitcher. Use wild boar, pork tenderloin, or venison backstrap: smoke it, grill it, or roast it. He always serves plenty of fresh-cut fruit or fruit salad with this hearty breakfast meal.

This is Jeff's "unbreakable Hollandaise" with a lime twist.

LIME-DAISE VARIATION ON UNBREAKABLE HOLLANDAISE

8 extra large egg yolks
2 tablespoons Hudson's on the Bend Champagne Herb Vinegar (www.hudsonsonthebend.com/store) or other wine vinegar
3 dashes Tabasco
juice of 2 limes
1 teaspoon salt, or to taste
1 pound butter
1 cup basil leaves, lightly packed

Combine all ingredients, except butter and basil leaves, in blender. Blend for 3 to 4 minutes at high speed.

Place butter in small saucepan over medium heat. Melt and heat to rolling boil.

With blender running on high, very slowly add boiling butter to the blender. Use a ladle, and add butter 1 ounce at a time. Adding hot butter all at once will make scrambled eggs, not sauce. If mixture becomes too stiff and will not blend, add 1 to 2 tablespoons of water to thin. Add basil and blend.

Store warm sauce in a thermal pitcher to maintain temperature. Sauce will break (separate) if reheated over direct heat.

Makes 2½ cups.

⁓

Jeff recommends using a stove-top smoker if you have one. And you can get one from his website, www.hudsonsonthebend .com/store, or at culinary equipment stores. Otherwise, grill or roast the pork. If you want to substitute venison backstrap, that works well, too.

SMOKED WILD BOAR, PORK, OR VENISON TENDERLOIN

2 wild boar or pork tenderloins or venison backstrap, approximately 16 ounces each
olive oil as needed
salt and pepper to taste

Lightly rub meat with olive oil. Season meat on all sides with salt and pepper. Grill over medium coals to medium rare, about 8 to 10 minutes. Or smoke in stove-top smoker (following manufacturer's instructions) for 8 to 10 minutes. Or roast in preheated 425° oven for 15–20 minutes or until medium rare (125°) on meat thermometer.

Cover with foil and let rest while poaching eggs. Finishing the assembled plates in oven will cook pork to medium (light pink in middle).

Makes 10 to 12 servings.

⁓

"We don't use fancy poachers," says Jeff. "We use a large pot with water and ½ cup vinegar to hold the eggs together while they are poaching." For many of us home cooks, an egg poacher would be a great help. Use one if you like.

To try his method at home, Jeff advises, "If you've not done this technique before, practice by poaching one or two eggs. If you are serving a large number of people, divide the final assembly into 2 or 3 shifts. Unless you are a pro at this procedure, poach no more than 8 eggs at a time." You've been advised . . . to get a "fancy poacher."

POACHED EGGS

water for poaching
½ cup white vinegar
20 eggs

Fill an 8-quart saucepan ⅔ full with water. Add ½ cup of white vinegar. Bring the water to a very light simmer and with a large slotted spoon, spin the water in a gentle "whirlpool" motion.

Crack up to 8 eggs at a time and drop the raw eggs, one by one, into the swirling water. Maintain this motion by gently stirring along the side of the pot. After 4 minutes, your eggs should be poached in a teardrop shape. Remove them from the water with a slotted spoon. Drain on cloth towels while poaching remaining eggs.

TO ASSEMBLE ELEMENTS OF DISH

Preheat oven to 375°. Heat plates while oven is preheating.
Place 2 pancakes per person (20) on unlined or foil-lined baking sheet. Slice the meat ¼ inch thick. Place 2 to 3 slices of meat on top of each pancake. Warm in preheated oven for 7 minutes. Remove from the oven.

For final assembly, place 2 potato pancakes on each heated plate. Place 1 poached egg atop meat slices arranged on each pancake. Ladle poached eggs with warm Lime-daise Sauce.

Makes 10 servings (2 eggs, 2 potato pancakes each).

Sylvia Casares

SYLVIA'S ENCHILADA KITCHEN, NO BORDERS

Houston

Sylvia's Enchilada Kitchen grew out of Sylvia Casares's love for the South Texas cuisine she grew up on in the lower Rio Grande Valley. Sylvia started her first restaurant in Rosenberg, a small town near Houston, after a successful career in research for a major food manufacturer. She opened her first Houston restaurant in 2001 and has since opened a second location and launched a food truck.

Known as the Enchilada Queen, Sylvia has brought her scientific rigor to the meticulous development of her recipes and menu. She makes 18 different sauces to drape over the stuffed and rolled tortillas that comprise her enchilada repertoire. Her food truck, No Borders, brings her food to the streets of Houston. She's made enchiladas an art as well as a science.

"Use fresh lard for best flavor," Sylvia advises. Prepare the husks by combining 2 bags of corn husks and a gallon of warm water in a large container. Weigh husks down to submerge and soak husks for at least an hour.

Sylvia's Pork Tamales

CHILE SAUCE

1 quart plus 3 cups water (divided use)
8 chile cascabel, seeds and stems removed

In a medium saucepan add water and chilies. Bring to a boil over high heat. Reduce heat and simmer for 15 minutes. Set aside and cool for about 15 minutes

In a blender, blend chilies with about 3 cups of water. Pour mixture through a colander to remove solids that did not liquefy. Set aside to add to masa dough.

PORK FILLING

15 pounds pork butt, well trimmed of fat
2½ quarts water
1 large onion, cut into quarters
1 whole head of garlic, rinse before adding to stockpot
2 teaspoons salt
¼ cup vegetable oil

Cut pork into 1-inch pieces. Combine pork with water, onion, garlic, and salt in a 10-quart stockpot. Bring to a

On December 24, my Mama Grande, Sarita Casares, would come to our home and she would be the matriarch in charge of the *tamalada* (tamale-making party) we had in my parents' home. She was in charge of preparing the masa and the meat, which meant making certain the flavors of both were to her standards. She was born in 1886 so she, of course, cooked only from scratch. My aunts and the kids would assemble to help with all parts of the production and in the evening we would gather around a table and eat all the fresh tamales we could possibly eat. My mother served them simply with fresh-made salsa, Mexican rice, charro beans, and guacamole. We all looked forward to the tamales and the love we shared in being one big happy, happy family!

—Sylvia Casares

boil over high heat. Reduce heat and simmer for about 90 minutes or until very tender.

Remove pork from pan and place in a large sauté pan. Set aside pork stock for later use. Add ¼ cup vegetable oil and sauté pork over medium heat until a little golden at the edges.

Cover and set aside in the refrigerator until ready to use for Pork Guisado Filling.

PORK GUISADO FILLING

> 25 chile cascabel, rinsed and stems removed
> 5 chile de arbol, stems removed
> 1 large onion, cut into quarters
> 2 quarts plus ¼ cup water (divided use)
> 4 cloves garlic
> Pork Filling (see recipe above)
> 1 teaspoon ground cumin
> 1 tablespoon ground oregano
> 1 teaspoon ground black pepper
> 2 tablespoons salt

Place chilies, onion, and water in a large stockpot. Bring to a boil over high heat. Reduce heat and simmer for about 30 minutes. Set aside and cool for about 15 minutes.

Using a food processor or a blender, blend the chilies, onion, and water to make a smooth sauce. Pour liquid through a colander to remove solids. Blend garlic cloves with ¼ cup water. Add to blended mixture.

Add blended guisado mixture to browned pork pieces. Stir in cumin, oregano, black pepper, and salt. Simmer 15 minutes. Set aside and cool for about 15 minutes before beginning tamale preparation. Adjust seasoning with salt.

MASA

> 7 pounds (28 cups) Maseca brand instant corn masa flour
> 2 tablespoons plus 2 teaspoons salt
> 2 tablespoons plus 1 teaspoon baking powder
> 4 pounds lard
> 6½ cups reserved pork stock
> 24 ounces Chile Sauce (p. 20)
> 8 cups water

Combine dry ingredients in a large bowl. Mix well by hand. Combine lard, pork stock, Chile Sauce, and water in a large saucepan. Heat over low heat to melt the lard, using a whisk to blend all the ingredients.

Add the liquid mixture to the dry ingredients (masa flour) about 3 cups at a time.

Mix all ingredients and knead until dough is well blended and light. This will require about 15 minutes of kneading by hand or, if using a mixer, blend about 10 minutes to 15 minutes.

Cover with plastic wrap and set aside.

TO SHAPE TAMALES

Assemble all prepared ingredients: masa dough, corn husks, pork guisado.

Place *about* 2 ounces of masa dough in the center of the corn husk.

With the back of a serving spoon (tablespoon) spread evenly almost to the very edges of the husk. The husk will resemble a triangle (wide on one end and narrow on the other). The masa should be spread from the wide end to approximately 4 inches toward the narrow end.

Place approximately 2 ounces (2 tablespoons) of pork guisado stuffing down the center of the masa.

Fold the sides of the husk one at a time toward the center. They will overlap.

Fold the bottom part of the husk (without the masa) up. Place tamale facedown in a container.

Repeat until all masa and stuffing are finished.

TO STEAM TAMALES

You will need a 40-quart stockpot with a rack. Place the rack and enough hot water to the top of the base. Place a coin in the water.

Place corn husks on the rack and then stack tamales on the rack forming a "tower" design. Cover the tamales with a layer of corn husks and a dish towel.

Cover the stockpot and cook tamales over low heat for about 1 hour and 30 minutes. If you hear the coin rattling, add more water.

After steaming tamales, turn off heat (leave pot on the burner) and allow to finish cooking for another 30 minutes.

Tamales should be cooked completely (husk should peel easily from dough).

Makes about 10 dozen tamales.

Robert Del Grande

RDG + BAR ANNIE, CAFÉ EXPRESS, THE GROVE, RIO RANCH, TACO MILAGRO, AVA BRASSERIE, PIZZERIA ALTO

Houston

Robert Del Grande ranks among the grand dons of Texas cuisine. He opened Café Annie in 1980 and along the way started Texas cuisine on an ascendant path. Robert, along with Dean Fearing and Stephan Pyles, independently and together developed what became known as Southwestern cuisine. A few years ago, Robert reinvented his signature restaurant as RDG + Bar Annie. It enjoys the same acclaim that made Café Annie a national dining destination during its thirty-year run.

He turned his considerable talents on fast casual dining to create Café Express and Taco Milagro. The Schiller Del Grande Restaurant Group (which includes founding partners Lonnie and Candice Schiller and Robert's wife, Mimi) has added a steakhouse, a Mediterranean brasserie, and a pizzeria to their stable.

With a PhD in biochemistry, Robert has always brought a rigor and precision to his food that guides his creativity and understanding of why things taste good.

The recipe described below uses a regular ham—actually a half bone-in ham, the type you usually see in supermarkets. An unsliced ham works best. A whole ham will also work nicely—you just need a bigger pot and more liquid to poach it in. If you're using a traditional salted and air-dried Kentucky or Tennessee ham, soak the ham overnight in water and then scrub it to clean it. Then very slowly simmer the ham in the biggest pot you can find. Not much can go wrong here. It's just a slow simmering of the ham. And lastly, the Christmas ham—while great for Christmas dinner—would make delicious appearances on the table throughout the week: in ham and eggs, biscuits and ham, ham sandwiches, etc., etc., etc.

Robert Del Grande's Christmas Country Ham with Grits and Cider Sauce

1 whole or half bone-in ham
2 quarts apple cider
2 quarts water
2 cups brown sugar
2 oranges, cut into quarters
2 tablespoons whole juniper berries
2 tablespoons whole coriander seeds
1 tablespoon black peppercorns
1 tablespoon fennel seeds
1 teaspoon whole cloves

Place ham in a pot large enough to easily hold the ham and all the liquid. Place ham in pot on stove. Add remaining liquid and seasoning ingredients. Turn heat to lowest setting so the liquid warms very slowly. The liquid should never boil, only simmer. It may take an hour or two to heat the liquid to a simmer, but the objective is to very slowly heat the ham so it absorbs the moisture and flavors of the liquid. Simmer ham until it reaches between 150° and 165° on an instant-read meat thermometer inserted in the thickest part.

Allow to cool somewhat for safer and easier handling. Carefully remove the ham from the liquid and place in a roasting pan. The ham can be held at room temperature until ready

Chef Robert Del Grande

to serve. The ham can be reheated in the oven with a glaze (see recipe below).

To serve the ham, slice thin. Traditional air-dried and salted country hams should be sliced very thin. Serve with RDG Holiday Grits and Cider Sauce.

Makes 10 to 20 servings.

GLAZE FOR COUNTRY HAM

¼ cup mustard
¼ cup molasses or maple syrup
1 teaspoon ground black pepper
¼ teaspoon ground cinnamon

Preheat oven to 375°. In a small bowl, combine mustard, molasses or syrup, pepper, and cinnamon. Brush ham with glaze. Roast ham until the glaze lightly caramelizes to a golden brown and the ham is heated through, about 30 minutes.

Makes ½ cup.

CIDER SAUCE FOR COUNTRY HAM

2 tablespoons butter
4 garlic cloves, finely chopped
½ white onion, finely chopped
2 cups cooking liquid reserved from ham
1 teaspoon whole juniper berries, lightly crushed
2 cups heavy cream
2 tablespoons Italian parsley, chopped
1 tablespoon fresh tarragon, chopped
salt and pepper to taste

In a medium saucepan, melt the butter over medium heat. Add garlic and onion; cook until translucent, stirring occasionally. Do not brown.

Add ham stock and juniper berries. Bring to a simmer and reduce liquid by half. When ready to serve, add the cream and chopped herbs; heat through. Adjust seasoning with salt and pepper.

Makes about 3 cups.

RDG HOLIDAY GRITS

2 quarts water
2 teaspoons salt
¾ cup coarse artisan grits
½ cup cream
4 tablespoons butter

Combine the water and salt in a large saucepan and bring to a boil over high heat.

Stir in the grits. Lower the heat and simmer until the grits are thick, about 30 to 35 minutes for coarse grits. If the grits become too thick, stir in additional water, thinning to desired consistency.

When ready to serve, stir in the cream and butter.

Makes 6 servings.

Dean Fearing

FEARING'S RESTAURANT

Dallas

Now at the helm of his eponymous restaurant at the Ritz-Carlton, Dallas, Dean is one of those Kentucky boys who got to Texas as fast as he could. Dean gained international fame at the Mansion on Turtle Creek in the go-go eighties. Along with Robert Del Grande and Stephan Pyles, Dean created and promoted the style of cooking that came to be known as Southwestern cuisine.

With several cookbooks, television shows, and a product line to his credit, Dean opened Fearing's Restaurant in 1997. Dean's signature dishes include the lobster taco and tortilla soup. He has a unique way of dipping into his grandmother's recipe box and coming out with an incredibly creative and sophisticated take on a timeless dish whether it's a riff on barbecue or chicken-fried Maine lobster.

Dean and his longtime friend, Robert Del Grande, are also known for their love of music. When these two get together

with their all-chefs band, the Barbwires, the music is as sweet as the cooking whether they're strumming guitars or banging pots and pans.

Tortilla–Corn Bread Dressing is Dean's Southwest adaptation of Granny Fearing's corn bread dressing that she used to make stuffing balls. Dean loves them "because they get crusty like the top of the dressing only all the way around. I had to get that idea from my grandmother. They were great. I don't want to think how much bacon grease hers probably had in them." This version is sans bacon grease. For full flavor, use Dean's Tortilla Broth, but in a pinch, turkey or chicken stock will do.

No childhood memories are as vivid to me as the memories from the food side of life. And my greatest food memories go back to holidays in Ashland, Kentucky. That's in eastern Kentucky.

My grandmothers on both sides of the family lived a few doors down. Both were country cooks who moved into town from the farm as they got older. They didn't have jalapeños, no dry rubs or spices like we take for granted. All they had was salt and pepper but everything I ever ate that they cooked was perfectly seasoned.

Both had big wooden dining room tables that would be covered with food: pies, cakes, at least three proteins, canned goods that had been brought up from the cellar. And they cooked all this on four-burner gas stoves, aprons tied around their waists, hair knotted in buns. They'd practically cook themselves to death so a full house of about 25 people could just mow down all the food. I know it took them at least three days. I can still remember the smell as soon as I walked in the door. Even at three or four, I knew I was going to have the best meal ever.

My sons have grown up eating holidays meals at the restaurant. That's great but it's nothing compared to the old days when everything was home-cooked from scratch.

—*Dean Fearing*

Dean Fearing's Tortilla–Corn Bread Dressing

vegetable oil
14 (6-inch) corn tortillas, halved and cut into strips ¼ inch wide
6 cups crumbled homemade (p. 18) or store-bought corn bread
2 tablespoons extra-virgin olive oil, plus more for the baking dish
1 large onion, chopped
2 celery ribs, chopped
2 garlic cloves, finely chopped
1 large jalapeño, seeded and finely chopped
1 tablespoon minced cilantro
2 teaspoons finely chopped fresh sage
2 teaspoons finely chopped fresh thyme
2 teaspoons chili powder
1 quart Tortilla Broth (see recipe below), or chicken or turkey stock
kosher salt to taste

In a large saucepan, heat 2 inches of vegetable oil to 350° over medium-high heat. Working in batches, fry the tortilla strips, stirring a few times, until golden and crisp, about 3 minutes. Using a slotted spoon, transfer the strips to paper towels to drain. Pour away vegetable oil. Place tortilla strips in a large bowl; add the corn bread.

Heat 2 tablespoons olive oil in the saucepan. Add onion and celery; cook over moderate heat, stirring, until softened, about 6 minutes. Add garlic and jalapeño; cook until fragrant, about 1 minute. Stir in cilantro, sage, thyme, and chili powder; cook until the chili powder is fragrant, about 1 minute.

Add broth and bring to a simmer over moderate heat. Pour the mixture over the tortilla strips and corn bread; season with salt to taste and toss gently to coat. Let stand until the broth has been absorbed, about 30 minutes.

Preheat the oven to 350°. Lightly oil a 9 × 13-inch baking dish. Transfer the dressing to the prepared dish and cover with foil. Bake for about 20 minutes, until heated through. Uncover and bake for about 15 minutes longer, until the top begins to brown.

Unbaked dressing may be refrigerated for up to 2 days. Bring to room temperature before baking.

Makes 12 servings.

To prepare Stuffing Balls: Instead of spreading dressing mixture into oiled baking dish, shape batter into 24 (½-cup) balls. Place in oiled baking dish. Leave space between the stuffing balls; do not allow sides to touch. Bake for 30 to 35 minutes until golden brown and crisp.

DEAN FEARING'S TORTILLA BROTH

3 tablespoons vegetable oil
2 (6-inch) corn tortillas, chopped
3 garlic cloves
1 medium onion, finely chopped
1 cup canned tomato puree
5 cups chicken or turkey stock
1 tablespoon chili powder
1 bay leaf
½ tablespoon ground cumin
pinch of cayenne pepper
salt to taste

Heat oil in a large saucepan over medium-high heat. Add chopped tortillas and garlic; cook, stirring occasionally, until tortillas are crisp and garlic is brown, about 3 minutes.

Add onion along with tomato puree and bring to a boil. Add stock, chili powder, bay leaf, and cumin and bring to a boil. Reduce heat to low and simmer until reduced to 1 quart, about 30 minutes. Discard bay leaf.

Working in batches, puree the mixture in a blender. Add a pinch of cayenne and season with salt.

Broth may be refrigerated for up to 3 days or frozen for 1 month.

This is Granny Fearing's homemade relish recipe adapted to add zing with jalapeño.

DEAN FEARING'S CRANBERRY-JALAPEÑO RELISH

1 orange
1 cup whole cranberries
2 teaspoons grated fresh ginger
2 teaspoons chopped fresh cilantro
2 teaspoons chopped jalapeño chili
maple syrup to taste

Peel zest from orange with a sharp potato peeler. Remove white pith and seeds from orange.

Combine orange zest and fruit, cranberries, ginger, cilantro, and jalapeño in a food processor. Pulse—turn on and off quickly—several times to coarsely chop. Do not puree. Or process fruit in a grinder fitted with medium die.

Turn chopped or ground fruit into a bowl. Add maple syrup and mix well. Cover and set aside for at least 30 minutes before using.

Store in refrigerator.

Makes 2 cups.

Johnny Hernandez

LA GLORIA ICEHOUSE, THE FRUTERIA, TRUE FLAVORS CATERING

San Antonio

Born into a San Antonio restaurant family, Johnny sought classic training at the Culinary Institute of America before returning home in 1994 and launching a catering business that has propelled him into the ranks of Texas celebrity chefs.

Johnny's La Gloria Icehouse, opened in 2010 on the grounds of the historic Pearl Brewery, brings some of Mexico's

authentic street-food flavors to Texas in an atmosphere that mirrors the historic intertwining of cultures arbitrarily separated by the Rio Grande. *Tlayudas* (Mexican pizzas on large flour tortillas), tacos, *sopes*, tostados, and quesadillas as well as grilled seafood transcend borders.

Johnny's latest venture, the Fruteria—Botanero, is a cultural as well as culinary adventure into Mexican *botanas*, or small plates. By day, the emphasis is on fruit cups, *licuados* (smoothies), tortas, and tostados. By night, the emphasis is on fruit-infused cocktails, tequila, and *antojitos* (Mexican appetizers).

Sweet dessert tamales are a must-have in many homes on Christmas Eve or anytime during the holidays. Kids traditionally wash them down with hot chocolate; adults with coffee or hot chocolate . . . spiked, if desired.

Johnny Hernandez's Tamales de Dulce (Sweet Tamales) with Pineapple

8 ounces dry corn shucks (soaked in water overnight)
5 cups Maseca brand instant corn masa flour for tamales
2 cups brown sugar
1 tablespoon baking powder
1 teaspoon salt
1 cup vegetable shortening
3 cups milk
15 ounces cream of coconut
1 cup golden raisins
1 cup toasted shredded coconut
2 cups Pineapple Filling (see recipe below)

Soak corn shucks in water a day ahead or overnight to soften until pliable.

In a large mixing bowl combine masa, brown sugar, baking powder, and salt; reserve.

Place shortening in a large mixing bowl and beat at high speed using an electric mixer until light and fluffy, about 3 to 5 minutes. Add dry ingredients to shortening in 3 to 4 batches, mixing well each time.

Remove bowl from mixer. Using a spoon, gradually stir in milk and cream of coconut, blending until thoroughly mixed. Fold in raisins and coconut; adjust seasoning with salt.

To assemble tamale: Place 3 tablespoons of masa (dough) mixture in the center bottom half of a soaked corn husk with the widest part of the husk facing you and the narrow side of the husk facing away. Place about 1 tablespoon pineapple filling in center of tamale, leaving dough around the edges.

Fold the shuck from left to right to form a tube of dough, then fold the top portion of the husk toward you so that it meets the bottom half. Filling should be sealed inside the dough and dough should be covered by the shuck.

To cook, stack tamales in a steamer on rack over hot water. Cook over simmering water for 30 to 45 minutes or until dough pulls away cleanly from the husk. Serve warm.

PINEAPPLE FILLING FOR TAMALES

2 cups finely chopped fresh pineapple
8 ounces *piloncillo* (unrefined Mexican sugar)
1 cinnamon stick
1 cup brown sugar
2 cups water

Combine chopped pineapple, *piloncillo*, cinnamon stick, brown sugar, and water in a medium saucepan over medium heat. Bring liquid to a boil; reduce heat and simmer approximately 30 minutes. Mixture should thicken to the consistency of thick syrup. Cool and use to fill tamales.

Reserve any remaining filling for another use.

Makes about 3 cups.

Tim Love

LONESOME DOVE WESTERN BISTRO,
WHITE ELEPHANT SALOON, THE LOVE SHACK,
WOODSHED SMOKEHOUSE, TLC CATERING

Fort Worth

Lonesome Dove Western Bistro introduced Texas (and far beyond) to Tim Love's "urban western cuisine" concept that has made him one of the state's celebrated cowboy chefs. He started in the historic Fort Worth Stockyards in 2000; his latest

venture, Woodshed, is along the banks of the Trinity River that runs through the city. In between, he preserved the legendary White Elephant Saloon as a watering hole and dance hall.

Just as Lonesome Dove is Tim's very sophisticated homage to chuckwagon cooking, Woodshed reflects his appreciation for slow smoking, hot grilling, and his skill at the execution thereof. He's also cloned a version of his Fort Worth burger bar, the Love Shack, in his hometown of Denton.

This native Texan lives the way he cooks, full flavored and to the limit.

Purple Chipotle Garlic Mashed Potatoes

10 purple potatoes (about 3 pounds), peeled and halved
3 cups heavy cream, heated but not boiling
4 tablespoons unsalted butter, melted
8 to 9 roasted garlic cloves, pureed*
6 tablespoons pureed chipotle pepper, or to taste
salt and pepper to taste

Place potatoes in medium-size pot with lid. Add just enough water to cover; place over high heat with lid on. When water boils, lower heat to a slow boil and cook until potatoes are tender and easily pierced with a fork, about 15 to 20 minutes.

Pour potatoes and water into colander to drain. Return potatoes to hot pot over residual heat for a few minutes to evaporate residual water, shaking pot occasionally. Combine hot cream and melted butter; reserve.

Place potatoes in large mixing bowl. Mash coarsely by hand using potato masher. Using electric mixer, gradually add 1 cup of cream and butter mixture and mix at high speed until smooth and well blended. Slowly add remaining cream while mixing on medium speed. Using a rubber spatula, fold in garlic and chipotle purees. Season to taste with salt and pepper.

Makes 6 to 8 servings.

*To roast garlic cloves: Preheat oven to 250°. Peel garlic cloves and place in a single layer in a small baking dish. Drizzle with olive oil. Bake for 15 minutes or until garlic is soft.

TEXAS PILGRIM'S PROGRESS

One of the most special holiday moments for me was when I took my son, Tannahill, on his first hunting trip before Thanksgiving. My father taught me to hunt and the experience of passing on this tradition to my own son was extraordinary. As icing on the cake, we brought home our family's Thanksgiving turkey. With the whole family in the kitchen cooking the meal, I was completely overwhelmed with gratitude. To accompany our wild turkey, I made Purple Chipotle Garlic Mashed Potatoes as a flavorful way to add some color to our Thanksgiving feast. This dish reminds me of that very special Thanksgiving.

—Tim Love

FOOD . . .
A LOVE STORY

When I married Matt Martinez, he promised me I'd never have to cook. He kept that promise during 40 years of marriage. I was the taster and his hardest critic. We always worked together. He was front of the house. I was back. He was the cook. I was the taster. Since he's been gone, I decided I have to get up every day to build on the legacy he left. On holidays, Matt would cook for our family. He'd work up a menu. We'd talk about it. He'd start the night before at the restaurant and get up early to finish. He did 100 percent of the meal; that was his way of showing us he loved and cared for us.

Generally, we gathered at [one of the restaurants] No Place or the Lakewood location. We'd have traditional menus and vary them. At Thanksgiving, we always had turkey, and sometimes something else like chicken-fried rabbit or roast beef as well. He made sure everyone's favorites were on the table, such as Mexican macaroni and mashed potatoes for a daughter-in-law.

Now that he's gone, we divvy up the dishes among the kids. But Matt's always with us.

—*Estella Martinez*

Estella and Matt Martinez Jr.

MATT'S RANCHO MARTINEZ

Dallas, Garland, Cedar Hill, Allen

The late Matt Martinez Jr. is quoted throughout this book, especially when it comes to Tex-Mex and barbecue. He was known as the "King of Tex-Mex," and was a wonderful friend and one of my go-to authorities on all things Texas and culinary during his amazing life. Born into a renowned restaurant family in Austin, Matt thanked his paternal grandfather for launching the family restaurant business. Once a soldier in Pancho Villa's army, Delfino Martinez escaped the Federales into Texas, where he opened Austin's first Tex-Mex restaurant, El Original, in 1925. The family has been in the restaurant business ever since, and Matt Jr. grew up working in his father's El Rancho in Austin.

Estella married into the restaurant family Martinez. Although she was promised by Matt that she'd never have to cook if she married him, she learned the food business from the beginning. They were a team during their 40 years of marriage. Since Matt's death in 2009, Estella has carried on his legacy. She's opened a new location of Matt's Rancho Martinez in Dallas and continued Matt's work to educate new generations of culinarians through the family's generosity and dedication to the Texas Restaurant Association's Education Foundation and the Greater Dallas Restaurant Association's education programs.

Matt wrote two cookbooks and developed a line of seasonings as well. The first edition of this book wouldn't have happened without his help and guidance. Estella carries on his generous tradition, always willing to share her wisdom and ideas.

This is a Martinez family favorite. Rum is optional. Or make two batches, one for the kids without alcohol and one with spirits for the grown-ups.

Martinez Family Sweet Potato Eggnog with Dark Rum

1 gallon prepared eggnog
2 cups mashed cooked or canned sweet potatoes
1 tablespoon brown sugar, crumbled
1 teaspoon cinnamon
½ teaspoon cayenne pepper
½ cup dark rum or to taste (optional)
peppermint schnapps
confectioners' sugar

Combine eggnog, sweet potatoes, brown sugar, cinnamon, and cayenne pepper and blend until smooth. If time allows, refrigerate for several hours to allow flavors to meld. Add dark rum to taste, mixing well.

When ready to serve, dip rims of glasses or punch cups in peppermint schnapps. Dip into confectioners' sugar to rim the glass. Pour or ladle eggnog into prepared glasses.

Makes 8 to 10 servings.

⌒

Tom Perini

PERINI RANCH STEAKHOUSE

Buffalo Gap

Tom Perini's steakhouse has been on his family's working ranch since 1983. Located in the small town of Buffalo Gap (population 463) near Abilene in West Texas, Perini Ranch Steakhouse isn't just another small-town cow palace. He's catered his "cowboy gourmet" style at events from one end of the country to the others and abroad.

Yet most of the time, Tom and wife, Lisa, can be found on or around the ranch doing what they love best, making great food for a whole bunch of folks who travel from nearby Abilene and around the state to enjoy his authentic chuckwagon style of cooking. Lisa ramrods the Buffalo Gap Wine & Food Summit on the ranch, which draws winemakers and guest chefs from far and wide.

Every holiday season, Federal Express assigns an extra plane to Abilene to make sure that all the orders for Perini's Mesquite Smoked Beef Tenderloin make it to the intended tables on time. The flavor and tenderness of this signature product has made the Perini name a holiday must for many households and corporate gift lists. It is truly a culinary work of art whether it's in the Perini Ranch Steakhouse dining room or yours.

GETTING LUCKY

Several years ago my wife, Lisa, and I celebrated New Year's Eve in California with friends, and we planned to prepare black-eyed peas to surprise everyone on New Year's Day. However, no luck in purchasing black-eyed peas in California—no one even knew what they were! Now, wherever we might travel over New Year's, we're prepared. We pack a small Crock-Pot, black-eyed peas with snaps, bacon drippings, and a jalapeño. We can guarantee a lucky New Year anywhere we might be!

—Tom Perini

Chef Tom Perini (photo by Mark Davis)

A gubernatorial appointee to the Texas Historical Commission, Perini is as passionate about the state's history as its cuisine. He believes the New Year's Day tradition of eating black-eyed peas for good luck dates to the Civil War. Southerners, who found little left in the wake of General Tecumseh Sherman's March to the Sea, felt lucky that Yankee soldiers wouldn't touch what they thought were cowpeas. That left plenty of black-eyed peas for everyone else. The Perinis add green "snaps," unshelled black-eyed pea pods, to the pot for color and texture.

Tom Perini's New Year's Day Black-Eyed Peas

¼ pound salt pork or bacon
¼ cup water plus additional water as needed
4 (8-ounce) packages frozen black-eyed peas
1 or 2 whole fresh jalapeños, or to taste
salt and pepper to taste

Slice the salt pork into ¼-inch slices, then cut slices into ¼-inch strips. Or cut bacon into ¼-inch pieces. In a cast-iron pot, combine salt pork or bacon pieces slowly with water and cook over low heat until the water evaporates and the salt pork or bacon is crisp and slightly browned. Remove the pork strips from the pan; discard.

There will be a salty residue and a small amount of pork drippings left in the pan. Add the black-eyed peas and enough water to barely cover the peas. Bring to a boil, then reduce heat to a simmer. Return pork to pan and cook on low heat for 20 minutes.

Add the jalapeño(s) and simmer about 30 minutes longer, until peas are very tender and have absorbed the flavor of the jalapeño. Season with salt and pepper to taste.

Makes 6 to 8 servings.

Monica Pope

SPARROW BAR AND COOKSHOP
(FORMERLY T'AFIA)

Houston

Monica Pope has been a high-profile chef in Houston for more than 20 years and has been a pioneer in the farm-to-fork movement. Her restaurants have included Boulevard Bistrot, the Quilted Toque, and t'afia. In late 2012, she rebooted her t'afia concept and reopened it as Sparrow Bar and Cookshop.

Chef Monica Pope (photo by Debora Smail, Reality Photography)

"Eat where your food lives" is her trademark and the name of her online interactive cookbook, http://chefmonicapope .keepercollection.com/. She sponsors the Saturday morning Midtown farmers' market in her restaurant parking lot. From experience and practice, she advises that truly great meals begin with a visit to a farmers' market.

She's often been called the Alice Waters of the Third Coast, a tribute to her commitment to local, sustainable products and those who grow and make them in the coastal prairie region around Houston.

NOT YO MAMA'S GREEN BEAN CASSEROLE

I've been making this recipe my whole life . . . or at least 32 years of it. It's a tradition that started many years ago, during one of my first and best jobs in the business at Karen's Fine Foods. I would eventually be employed at Karen's on and off for about a decade—and even became the chef there, too, when I moved back to Houston to pursue my dream of opening my own restaurant. While I've always worked the holidays, as did my mother, who was a church organist for 50 years, we always made the time to share a wonderful family meal together. My mom would make her famous stuffing with Stouffer's stuffing mix, water chestnuts, green olives, and sausage, and I began bringing the green beans. They're easy and light—a perfect complement to rich holiday food—and while the dish is simple, it's just good eating that reinforces core principles that still resonate with me: fresh and local.

—*Monica Pope*

Monica Pope's Green Beans with Caramelized Shallots and Toasted Almonds

1 pound Harvester (heirloom) or haricots verts (French) green beans
2 to 3 shallots, peeled and sliced thin
1 tablespoon butter
1 teaspoon sugar
1 teaspoon red wine vinegar
½ cup blanched almonds, thinly sliced
1 tablespoon LeBlanc almond oil, or to taste
¼ cup freshly grated Parmesan
kosher salt and freshly ground black pepper to taste

Steam green beans just until tender, about 4 to 6 minutes. Drain and rinse with ice water to stop cooking.

Place shallots in small skillet over low heat with butter. When butter bubbles and shallots begin to brown at edges, add sugar and stir to coat well. When sugar has dissolved, stir in vinegar. Cook another minute or two, then remove from heat and reserve.

Place almonds in a dry skillet over medium heat. Cook just until edges begin to brown, 2 to 3 minutes. Be careful to avoid burning. Remove from heat and reserve.

To serve, reheat green beans, tossing with almond oil, in large skillet. Add shallots, stirring to incorporate. Turn out onto serving dish. Garnish with toasted almonds and Parmesan cheese. Season to taste with salt and pepper.

Makes 4 to 6 servings.

Stephan Pyles

STAMPEDE 66, STEPHAN PYLES RESTAURANT, SAMAR BY STEPHAN PYLES, STEPHAN PYLES CATERS, SKY CANYON, SKY CANYON WINE BAR

Dallas

For a kid who grew up working in his family's far West Texas truck stop café, Stephan Pyles has done right well for himself. Along with Robert Del Grande and Dean Fearing, Stephan was at the forefront of the Southwestern cuisine movement in the eighties. His Stampede 66, which opened in 2012, is an amazing hybrid of truck-stop cooking and avant-garde molecular cuisine.

Stephan first gained national recognition at his former Routh Street Café where his brand of Southwest cuisine was born. Although he ventures into other cuisines (lots of Mediterranean and South American at his namesake restaurant and Indian at Samar), Stephan just can't quit his Texas roots. He's got at least four lauded cookbooks to his name, as well as a Stampede 66 line of sauces.

Not one to let his résumé go to his head, Stephan never forgets that he grew up on his grandmother's honey-fried chicken. In fact, he's done his best to replicate it using a sous-vide technique at his newest restaurant.

⁓

His special dessert will make your Texas holiday heart sing.

Stephan Pyles' Peanut Butter–Banana Cream Pie with Hot Fudge

¼ cup banana liqueur
1½ teaspoons powdered gelatin
2¾ cups milk
½ vanilla bean, halved and scraped
4 eggs, separated
1½ cups sugar (divided use)
3 tablespoons cornstarch
2 ripe bananas (divided use)
juice of ½ of a lemon
¼ cup smooth peanut butter, at room temperature
1 9-inch baked pie crust (p. 33–34)
¾ cup chopped roasted peanuts (divided use)
pinch of salt
pinch cream of tartar
Hot Fudge Sauce (recipe follows)

Place the banana liqueur in a small mixing bowl; sprinkle the gelatin on top and allow to soften for 5 minutes. Place the bowl over simmering water until the gelatin on top is completely clear. Set aside.

In a saucepan, combine the milk and vanilla bean. Bring to a boil; remove from heat, cover, and allow to steep while preparing the yolk mixture.

In a mixing bowl, whisk the egg yolks while gradually adding ¾ cup of the sugar. When the yolks have lightened, whisk in the cornstarch. Strain the milk and gradually pour in the yolk mixture while stirring. Return to a clean saucepan set over medium heat, and stir constantly until the mixture begins to boil. Reduce the heat and continue to stir for 1 to 2 minutes. Remove from the heat, whisk in the gelatin, and incorporate thoroughly. Allow the pastry cream to cool completely.

Slice the banana on the bias and brush with lemon juice. Whip the peanut butter to make it easier to spread, then spread on top of the pie crust. Sprinkle half the peanuts on top of the peanut butter. Arrange half the banana slices on top of the peanuts and spread the pastry cream over the bananas. Arrange the remaining banana slices over the pastry cream, and then sprinkle the remaining peanuts on top of the bananas. Refrigerate while making the meringue.

Preheat the oven to 400°. Place the egg whites in a mixing bowl with the salt and cream of tartar. Beat with an electric mixer until soft peaks form. Gradually add the remaining ¾ cup sugar while beating, until soft peaks form and the meringue becomes glossy. Spread the meringue on top of the pie or place in a pastry bag and pipe decoratively. Make sure the meringue touches the pie shell all over.

Place the pie in the oven for no more than 1 minute. Watch constantly, and remove when the meringue is lightly browned. Refrigerate for at least 30 minutes before cutting.

Serve slices drizzled with Hot Fudge Sauce.

Makes 8 to 10 servings.

CREAM PIE, DREAM PIE

I practically grew up in my family's truck-stop café in Big Spring, where my mother made many of the pies, cakes, and cobblers. In my mind, her most remarkable accomplishments were her cream pies. Of all the pies she ever produced, none brings back such nostalgia as her banana cream pie with mile-high toasted meringue. We finished off our feasts with it at every Thanksgiving and Christmas that I can remember. With a fondness for the combination of banana, peanuts, and chocolate, I improvised on her classically beautiful concept to come up with a creation that satisfied my craving for the sweet "holy trinity." Now one of my dessert classics has become Peanut Butter–Banana Cream Pie with Hot Fudge.

—*Stephan Pyles*

STEPHAN PYLES' HOT FUDGE SAUCE

⅓ cup light corn syrup
¼ cup water
¾ cup sugar
¼ cup unsweetened cocoa powder
1 tablespoon chopped unsweetened chocolate
2 tablespoons unsalted butter
⅓ cup heavy cream

In a small saucepan, boil the syrup for 1 minute. Remove from heat and carefully stir in the water; use caution, as the mixture may splatter.

In a mixing bowl, sift together the sugar and cocoa. Stir into the corn syrup mixture. Bring to a bowl, stirring until the sugar is dissolved. Add the chocolate and butter, and whisk until melted. Add the cream and return to a boil. Remove from the heat.

The sauce can be made a day ahead; reheat gently.

Makes about 2 cups.

Grady Spears

GRADY'S LINE CAMP STEAKHOUSE

Tolar

You have to talk "cowboy" to understand the name of Grady Spears's new place. "Line camp" means a crude shack or even a dugout on the outermost ranch boundary where "line riders" patrolled to prevent rustling and keep the herd in bounds. No doubt most line riders never experienced food as good as Grady turns out.

He draws on the national soft drink of Texas, Dr Pepper, to braise short ribs and, of course, he turns out a chicken-fried steak that hangs over the edges of the plate. Grady calls himself

a cowboy cook instead of a chef. He didn't know he could cook all that well until he took a cooking shift at the Gage Hotel in Marathon (way out toward the Big Bend) when the chef was a no-show.

Grady's best known for his stints at restaurants Reata and the Chisholm Club. The Fort Worth native is close to home since opening Line Camp in 2011. He's on a stretch of State Highway 377, about 45 miles southwest in a little town called Tolar.

This recipe uses *piloncillo*, found in Hispanic groceries or supermarkets with imagination and depth. Unrefined sugar pressed into a cone shape, *piloncillo* tastes like molasses-flavored brown sugar even though there's no molasses in it. In order to use *piloncillo*, you must break it up by grating or chopping. If the cone is too hard to handle, pop it in the microwave for 10 to 20 seconds to soften.

Grady Spears' Beef Tenderloin with Cowboy Coffee Rub

1 (4- to 5-pound) beef tenderloin
1 cup grated *piloncillo* (unrefined Mexican sugar)
1 tablespoon kosher salt
1 tablespoon coarsely ground black pepper
⅛ cup ground coffee
2 tablespoons olive oil, or as needed

If tenderloin is untrimmed, remove the silvery skin. Use a paper towel to help get a hold on the skin while using a knife to peel it away from the meat. Trim any excess fat or loose pieces. Trim ends or tuck ends under to make a uniform-size piece of meat.

Combine grated *piloncillo*, salt, pepper, and coffee in a small bowl, mixing well. Rub tenderloin all over with olive oil. Coat the tenderloin evenly on all sides and ends with the coffee rub. Allow meat come to room temperature while heating coals to grill or preheating oven to roast.

To grill tenderloin: Heat coals to medium hot. Grill roast on all sides until light brown and caramelized. Move away from high heat and finish cooking over low coals. Allow 15 minutes per pound of meat. Cook until meat thermometer registers 120° in thickest part. Cover and let rest for 15 minutes.

To oven roast tenderloin: Position rack in the center of the oven and preheat to 250°. Place beef in shallow roasting pan. Roast in oven for 15 minutes per pound until meat thermometer registers 120° in thickest part. Cover and let rest for 15 minutes.

Slice tenderloin ½ inch thick.

Makes 8 servings.

Array of Texas spirits: (left to right) craft beer, vodka, whiskey, red wine, tequila, white wine.

In the Spirit of Texas: Wines, Beers, and Distilled Spirits

When the first edition of this book was published in 1998, the Texas wine industry was often summed up—and dismissed—as Chateau Bubba, a stereotype held by many consumers inside, as well as outside, the state, and certainly by a preponderance of national and international aficionados. Longnecks were about as artisanal and crafty as beer got. Distilling, to the extent that it existed, was a hobby or a crime, depending on whether the maker of the booze sold it.

Fifteen years later, the Texas wine industry is recognized as a significant economic force producing some damn good wines. Craft beers are ascendant in terms of quality and the numbers of breweries. More and more Texas distillers make and sell vodka; whiskeys, including bourbon and rye; gin; rum; liqueurs; and tequila. Even sake is now part of the Texas adult beverage world, with the opening of a *kura* (sake brewery) in 2011.

It is now as possible in Texas to "drink local" as it is to "eat local."

Texas Wines

North American, not just Texas, wine-making history dates to 1662 when Franciscan priests established a vineyard at the Ysleta mission near El Paso in what is now the wine-growing region designated as Mesilla Valley, one of eight recognized appellations or American Viticultural Areas (AVAs) in the state. An appellation isn't just about location or geography; it factors in climate, elevation, and soil.

Texas is now the fifth-largest wine-making state in the country with almost 300 wineries. Most of that growth has occurred in the past 20 years led by pioneers such as Becker Vineyards, Fall Creek Vineyards, La Buena Vida Vineyards, Llano Estacado Winery, and Ste. Genevieve Wines.

Besides producing wine, jobs, and tax revenue, Texas wineries have become destinations as well. "Wine Trails" attract visitors all over the state, in each of the five major wine-making

Texas has eight recognized appellations or American Viticultural Areas (AVAs):

Texas High Plains: West of Lubbock in the Panhandle at an elevation of 3,000–4,000 feet, the climate of this appellation is very dry.

Escondido Valley: This appellation established in 1992 covers 50 square miles in Pecos County in far West Texas, located near Fort Stockton.

Texas Hill Country: West of Austin and San Antonio, this appellation is the second-largest AVA in the United States with more than nine million acres. Two smaller appellations, listed below, have been designated within the Texas Hill Country in recognition of the unique microclimates they embody. Many wineries are located in this scenic area.

Bell Mountain (within Texas Hill Country): Designated in 1986, it is the first established AVA in Texas, covering five square acres about 15 miles north of Fredericksburg.

(*Continued next page*)

(*Continued from previous page*)

Fredericksburg (within Texas Hill Country): This viticultural area covers about 110 acres with approximately 60 under vine.

Mesilla Valley: Located at the far western tip of the Texas border north and west of El Paso, this area is hot and dry with a long growing season.

Texas Davis Mountains: This West Texas appellation is cool and wet at an elevation ranging from 4,500 to 8,300 feet.

Texoma: In north-central Texas, this area abuts the Texas-Oklahoma border.

Source: The U.S. Department of Treasury, Alcohol and Tobacco Tax and Trade Bureau

regions designated by the Texas Wine and Grape Growers Association. The scenic Texas Hill Country has the most vibrant wine tourism industry.

Besides growing in number, Texas wines have gained recognition. Top sommeliers and chefs include Texas wines on their lists. Retailers such as Central Market and Spec's devote shelf space and marketing to highlight Texas wines.

Winemakers and grape growers, in Texas as in any other geography and climate, face common challenges as well as circumstances unique to their area. Part of this learning curve has been discovering, through lots of trial and error, which grapes do best in Texas. Our warm (make that hot as hell) weather favors grapes that thrive in similar climates, such as Spanish Tempranillo, French Viognier, and Italian Sangiovese. Cooler weather varietals, such as Chardonnay, Cabernet Sauvignon, Merlot, and Pinot Noir thrive in more temperate climes such as in California, Washington State, and Oregon.

Gaining the self-assurance to grow and make wines from Spanish, southern French, and Italian grapes has been part of the maturing of the Texas wine industry.

In the late 1980s (and again in the 2010s), many people in the world associated Dallas with a television show by the same name, which starred a certain "villain" known as J.R. Ewing. I had the pleasure of serving dinner to the late Larry Hagman at Routh Street Café (Stephan Pyles's Dallas restaurant of the era) on a somewhat regular basis during the show's first incarnation when he was filming the TV show on-site here. He came in quite often.

On his very first visit however, I was determined that he try one of our burgeoning Texas wines that we were so proud of. And being a Texan himself, I was sure he would be interested. One of our finest vintages of that time was a 1981 Cabernet Sauvignon from Pheasant Ridge Winery. Robert Mondavi had earlier tasted it at a luncheon I prepared with the Texas Department of Agriculture in San Francisco and had mistaken it for a first-growth Bordeaux. So I confidently poured Mr. Hagman a glass at his table and told him to swirl the wine and smell its fragrance.

I said that since the grapes were produced in the high plains of Lubbock, he might detect a bit of "West Texas dustiness" in the nose. He swirled the wine, took a big sniff, looked at me squarely, and said, "Son, that's not dust, it's cow shit."

—*Stephan Pyles*

Texas Craft Beers

Longneck beers, such as Lone Star (1884) and Pearl (1886), are iconic symbols of Texas every bit as much as cowboy hats and boots. Since the 1990s, smaller-production regional and craft beers in Texas and across the country have been expanding in number and capacity to meet a growing demand. According to the Brewers Association, Texas is home to the country's fourth-largest craft beer maker, Spoetzl Brewery, known for Shiner Bock. Although located in the little Hill Country town of Shiner (between San Antonio and Houston), some would argue Spoetzl Brewery isn't exactly a small craft brewer, with distribution in more than 40 states. Whether it's called a craft or regional beer, Spoetzl is no newcomer. Founded in 1909, Spoetzl has brewed Shiner Bock since 1913.

Craft beers, defined as brews made by small regional breweries producing no more than two million barrels annually (for most a lot less), began to take off around the United States and in Texas in the 1990s. Even during the economic downturn of the late 2000s, sales of more expensive craft beers increased while sales of mass-produced beers that cost less declined.

Saint Arnold Brewing Company in Houston claims to be the state's oldest craft brewery, shipping its first keg in 1994. Certainly it is a leader in the modern era of craft beer making in the state. Before Saint Arnold, Houston was the largest city in the country that did not have a microbrewery. Since then brewers have proliferated all over the state, particularly in the Austin area. Some other well-known Texas craft beers include Deep Ellum Brewing, Dallas; Franconia Brewing, McKinney; Jester

TEXAS WINE-MAKING REGIONS

Region 1: High Plains with 5 wineries and 20 vineyards

Region 2: North Texas with 26 wineries and 25 vineyards

Region 3: East Texas and the Gulf Coast with 16 wineries and 14 vineyards

Region 4: West Texas with 3 wineries and 4 vineyards

Region 5: Central Texas and the Texas Hill Country with 38 wineries and 25 vineyards

Source: Texas Wine and Grape Growers Association (2013)

King Craft Brewing, Austin; Karbach Brewing, Houston; Real Ale Brewing, Blanco; and Southern Star Brewing, Conroe.

The Texas Craft Brewers Guild includes both breweries and brew pubs, also a growing category in Texas and the nation. For beer crafters, the brew isn't just about taste and convenience, it's about appreciation of the beverage, that is, beer culture. What's more Texas than that?

Texas Spirits

When it comes to hard liquor, Tito's Handmade Vodka is hard to beat. Founded by Tito Beveridge in 1997, Tito's has become a nationally recognized brand. (I promise, Beveridge really is his name.) The success of this brand emboldened other distillers to make vodka, particularly if they had access to water from underground springs (Dripping Springs and Savvy vodkas, for example). Texas distillers have gone on to make a veritable back bar of spirits: bourbon-style corn as well as rye whiskeys; gin; liqueurs; rum; tequila; and sake. The latter technically isn't a spirit because it is fermented, not distilled. Sake is sometimes called a rice wine, but that isn't accurate either since sake is made by a process similar to the way beer is brewed—using rice, water, and yeast—than to the way wine ferments beginning with grape juice. Whatever! It's made by the Texas Sake Company in Austin.

Despite Tito's success, spirits production in Texas got off to a slow start. In 2003, Paula Angerstein came out with Paula's Texas Lemon and Paula's Texas Orange liqueurs. The former is similar to Italian limoncello, the later to triple sec. In 2007, the spirit world exploded. Texas microdistillers introduced additional vodkas and Railean and Treaty Oak rums. Garrison Brothers and Balcones distilleries have come online with bourbon-style corn whiskeys. Roxor Artisan and Waterloo Handcrafted Texas Style gins are in the mix.

Where's the tequila, you ask? There are several tequilas marketed by Texas-based companies, starting with Republic Tequila in 2008. But to be called tequila, the liquor must be made in Mexico from blue agave plants raised in the state of Jalisco. No matter, marketing has created some "Texas-brand" tequilas, including Ambhar and Dos Lunas. Railean, the same distiller that produces rum, launched El Perico Agave Spirit in 2011. Because it is made in San Leon, Texas, it can't be called tequila even though it is made from blue agave, and bottled in two styles, silver and *reposado*. Sounds a lot like tequila!

Compared to the Texas wine and craft beer makers, micro-distillers in the state are just getting started, but they all make spirited statements. Try out some of these Texas-style cocktails using Texas wines, beers, and spirits.

The ultimate Texas variation on this classic cocktail uses tequila (Bloody Maria) instead of vodka (Bloody Mary).

Marfaschino Manhattan, p. 220; Texas Tea, p. 222; Mexican Martini, p. 223

Of course, you can make a pitcher full as well as by the glass. Make it with beer and it's a Michelada.

Tomato juice (or tomato juice with clam) is the backbone of several cocktails that make great brunch cocktails. They are also known for smoothing the edges of a hangover. Happy holidays!

My friend Pete Mitchell, bar owner par excellence in Houston (Leon's Lounge and Under the Volcano), serves a meal-in-a-glass Bloody Mary. Besides all the traditional garnishes, he adds a ⅛-inch-thick slice of summer sausage. Fabulous! This is my adaptation.

Bloody Maria or Mary

1½ ounces tequila or vodka
1 teaspoon horseradish
3 dashes red pepper sauce
3 dashes Worcestershire sauce
squeeze of lime juice
3 shakes celery salt
cracked black pepper to taste
3 ounces chilled tomato juice, or as needed
Garnishes: slice of summer sausage, celery stalk, pickled
  okra, pickled jalapeño, olives, cucumber stick,
  lemon and/or lime wedge, or any desired combination
  or variation

Place ice cubes in a highball glass to fill about ¾. Add tequila or vodka along with other ingredients except tomato juice. Fill glass with tomato juice. Mix by pouring back and forth into a cocktail shaker. Pour mixed drink and ice into a salt-rimmed (if desired) highball glass. Garnish as desired.

Makes 1 cocktail.

Bloody Maria or Mary by the Pitcher

1 (46-ounce) can tomato juice
2 tablespoons prepared horseradish
2 to 3 tablespoons lime juice
1 tablespoon celery salt
1 tablespoon ground black pepper
2 tablespoons Worcestershire sauce
1 to 2 tablespoons red pepper sauce
ice
12 ounces tequila or vodka, or as desired
Garnishes: celery stalk, pickled okra, pickled jalapeño,
   olives, cucumber stick, lemon or lime wedge, or
   combination

In large pitcher, combine tomato juice, horseradish, lime juice, celery salt, black pepper, Worcestershire sauce, and red pepper sauce. Stir well. Refrigerate at least an hour to chill.

To make drinks, fill a highball glass with ice; add 1½ ounces tequila or vodka or to taste. Fill with Bloody Maria or Bloody Mary mixer. Blend by pouring contents back and forth into a cocktail shaker. Garnish as desired.

Makes 6 to 7 cocktails.

The Michelada is a Bloody made with beer.

Michelada

1 teaspoon horseradish
3 dashes red pepper sauce
3 dashes Worcestershire sauce
squeeze of lime juice
3 shakes celery salt
cracked black pepper to taste
6 ounces chilled tomato juice, or as needed
1 (12-ounce) beer
lemon or lime wedge

Place ice cubes in a highball glass to fill about ¾. Add all ingredients except beer and lemon or lime wedge. Mix by pouring back and forth into a cocktail shaker. Pour tomato mixture into a chilled salt-rimmed (if desired) beer mug or schooner. Add beer to fill. Garnish with lemon or lime. Serve with bottle of remaining to refill as desired.

Makes 1 serving.

There's not a lot of difference between the *cerveza preparada*, or "prepared beer," and *chavela*. Both are tomato juice and beer cocktails, with less folderol than the Michelada. Around the frat house or the hunting lodge, they're simply called Red Beer.

Cerveza Preparada or Chavela

3 ounces tomato juice
6 dashes hot red pepper sauce
1 (12-ounce) bottle pale lager
lemon wedge
1 side shot (1½ ounces) tequila, optional

Salt the rim of a beer mug or lager glass; fill with ice. Add tomato juice, hot sauce, and beer to fill. Drop in the lemon wedge. Serve with remaining beer, which should be used to refill the glass. Serve with a side shot of tequila, if desired.

Makes 1 cocktail.

This cocktail is refreshing but with a kick and named after one of the state's iconic songs. Go really regional with Topo Chico sparkling mineral water, from Mexico. I confess that the first time I saw bottles of Topo Chico on a grocery store shelf in Texas, I thought I'd seen a punch line in search of a joke. After all, when gringos go to Mexico, the number one rule is: Don't drink the water. That's still true about tap water south of the border, but Topo Chico is the real deal and great as a mixer or straight out of the longneck bottles in which it is sold.

Yellow Rose of Texas

2 ounces orange juice
1 ounce rye whiskey or bourbon
½ ounce tequila
Topo Chico Agua Mineral or other sparkling water

Place ice cubes in lowball glass to fill about halfway. Add orange juice, whiskey, and tequila. Add a splash of sparkling water or as much as desired. Stir to combine ingredients.

Makes 1 cocktail.

This concoction melds the traditional flavors of West Indies rum punch with prickly pear soda, making it a very Texas way to celebrate the holidays on Padre Island or anywhere along Texas Gulf Coast. Prickly pear is the beautiful purple-red fruit of the nopales cactus with a fruity taste and vibrant color similar to watermelon.

Texas Rum Punch

1 cup fresh lime juice
2 cups Italian prickly pear soda
3 cups dark or light rum
2 cups orange juice
2 cups pineapple juice
4 dashes bitters
freshly grated nutmeg

In a pitcher, combine lime juice, soda, rum, orange and pineapple juice. Add a few dashes of bitters and some grated nutmeg to taste. Serve chilled over ice.

Makes 10 to 12 cocktails.

While sipping a Manhattan at the bar at Jett's Grill in Marfa's historic Hotel Paisano, some friends and I decided we'd henceforth refer to the cocktail's garnish as Marfaschino cherries. It's become our New Year's celebration "thang," especially when we are in this great Big Bend town.

Marfaschino Manhattan

2 ounces rye whiskey or bourbon
½ ounce sweet vermouth
2 to 3 dashes Angostura bitters
ice
maraschino cherry, for garnish

Pour the ingredients into a cocktail shaker with ice cubes. Shake well. Strain into a chilled lowball glass, without or with rocks. Garnish with the cherry.

Makes 1 cocktail.

People used to think that margaritas came from machines. And a lot of them do. More and more, real margarita lovers demand theirs on the rocks instead of frozen. There are almost as many margarita mixes as Bloody Mary mixes on the market, but the secret to a great margarita isn't just the height of the shelf the tequila bottles rest on. Great margaritas on the rocks require fresh lime juice, good quality (that is, top-shelf) tequila, AND orange-flavored liqueur that gives the drink its sparkle. Triple Sec or Grand Marnier are traditional. But just try a margarita with a dash of Paula's Texas Orange or Lemon Liqueur, made in Austin.

A Real Margarita

½ cup fresh lime juice
½ cup tequila
½ cup orange-flavored liqueur or brandy
lime wedges

Combine lime juice, tequila, and orange liqueur in a large cocktail shaker or a pitcher with ice. Shake or stir to mix and chill. Strain into salt-rimmed, chilled cocktail glasses, with or without ice. Garnish with lime wedges.

Makes 3 servings.

Grapefruit is the winter fruit for which Texas is best known. Okay, peaches are pretty Texas, too, but not for the winter holidays. Hence the emphasis on grapefruit drinks. And if you've never had a Rio Red or Rio Star grapefruit from the Lower Rio Grande Valley, you are missing the real deal. This cocktail is a tribute to Texas grapefruit and tequila.

La Paloma

2 ounces tequila
Italian grapefruit soda or lemon-lime soda
juice of wedge of lime
dash of salt

Fill salt-rimmed (optional) collins glass with ice and pour tequila over ice. Add grapefruit or lemon-lime soda. Squeeze fresh lime into cocktail. Add a dash of salt if not using salt-rimmed glasses.

Makes 1 cocktail.

No rundown of cocktails with Texas roots would be complete without a Greyhound (vodka or gin and grapefruit juice) and a Salty Dog. Basically the same cocktail, the latter is served in a glass with a salted rim. This cocktail is the most fun way to use all those beautiful Ruby Red or Ruby Star grapefruit that came in the holiday gift box. I added some agave liqueur to the recipe to give the cocktail a touch of sweet. I particularly like Jose Cuervo's Agavero, made from *reposado* and *anejo*, tequilas aged in oak barrels.

To salt the rims of cocktail glasses: Pour a thin layer of sea salt, coarse or kosher salt into a saucer. Rub rim of chilled cocktail glass with lemon, lime, or grapefruit wedge, then dip rim in salt.

Texas Greyhound or Salty Dog

1½ ounces gin or vodka
4 ounces grapefruit juice, or as desired
splash of agave liqueur
1 wedge grapefruit

For a Salty Dog, salt the rim of a highball or collins glass. Fill glass (with or without salted rim) with ice cubes. Pour gin or vodka and grapefruit juice over ice. Top off with a splash of agave liqueur. Garnish with wedge of grapefruit.

Makes 1 cocktail.

⁓

This sparkling wine cooler marries for life with the delicious flavor of limoncello. It makes a beautiful holiday cocktail in a champagne flute.

Texas Lemon Sparkler

1 ounce Paula's Texas Lemon liqueur or limoncello, well-chilled
champagne or sparkling wine, well chilled
mint sprig

Pour lemon liqueur or limoncello into champagne flute. Top with champagne or sparkling wine. Garnish with mint sprig.

Makes 1 cocktail.

⁓

This potent concoction uses all the major Texas spirits. Make sure there's a designated driver.

Texas Tea

2 ounces tequila
2 ounces rum
2 ounces vodka
2 ounces gin
2 ounces bourbon
2 ounces orange or lemon liqueur
3 cups sweet tea or as needed

Fill a 1-gallon pitcher with ice. Add tequila, rum, vodka, gin, bourbon, and liqueur. Stir, then add tea to top off the pitcher. Pour into highball or iced tea glasses with ice.

Makes 6 to 8 cocktails.

⁓

The origins of this truly Texas cocktail—more than a little dirty (with olive juice and olives)—can be traced back to one of the state's legendary bars, the Cedar Door in Austin. The original as well as variations are the official unofficial drink of the state capital. Now they're all over the state and the nation. Here's my version.

Mexican Martini

2 ounces silver tequila
2 ounces orange liqueur or orange brandy
1 ounce orange juice
1 ounce lime juice
splash of olive juice or to taste
olives

Pour tequila, orange liqueur or brandy, and juices over crushed ice in a cocktail shaker. Shake vigorously to blend. Strain into chilled martini glass. Garnish with skewered olives.

Makes 1 large or 2 modest martinis.

⁓

Yet another delicious use for prickly pear soda, a light pink sparkling soft drink, made from the fruit of the nopales cactus.

Prickly Pear Margarita Martini

2 ounces silver tequila
1 ounce orange liqueur
3 ounces Italian prickly pear soda
2 ounces lime juice
1 cup crushed ice
lime wedge, for garnish

Combine ingredients in a cocktail shaker. Shake and strain into chilled martini glass. Or combine ingredients over ice in a lowball glass; mix well. Garnish with lime wedge.

Makes 1 cocktail.

⁓

Wine punch, Spanish-style, translates well to party time in Texas. Serve it in a punch bowl or a large pitcher.

Red Sangria

1 bottle dry red wine, chilled
¼ cup lemon juice or juice from one lemon
⅓ cup orange juice or juice from one orange
4 tablespoons sugar or ¼ cup simple syrup, or to taste
2 ounces brandy, orange or lemon liqueur
chilled sparkling mineral water, club soda, or ginger ale,
   as desired
slices of lemon and lime

In large pitcher, combine wine and lemon and orange juices. Add sugar or simple syrup and brandy or liqueur. Stir to blend. Chill several hours. To serve, pour sangria mixture over ice in collins or highball glasses. Top off with sparkling mineral water, club soda, or ginger ale, as desired.

Garnish with lemon and lime slices.

Makes 4 to 5 servings.

Here's a variation on the sangria theme, using white wine.

White Sangria

⅔ cup simple syrup or sugar, or to taste
3 oranges, sliced
1 lemon, sliced
1 lime, sliced
1 bottle white wine, chilled
2 ounces brandy, orange or lemon liqueur
chilled sparkling mineral water, club soda, or ginger ale,
   as desired
white grapes
mint leaves

In large pitcher, combine simple syrup or sugar with orange, lemon, and lime slices. Allow to meld for at least an hour or until sugar is dissolved. Add wine and brandy or liqueur. Chill several hours. To serve, pour sangria mixture over ice in collins

Simple syrup is the bartender's friend, as well the sweet-tea maker's best buddy. The utility of simple syrup is that the sugar is completely dissolved for easy mixing.

To make simple syrup: Combine 1 cup water and 1 cup sugar in a small saucepan. Bring to a boil, stirring, until sugar has dissolved. Allow to cool. Makes 1½ cups.

1 ounce simple syrup = 1 teaspoon sugar = 1 sugar cube

or highball glasses. Top off with sparkling mineral water, club soda, or ginger ale, as desired.

Garnish with white grapes and mint leaves.

Makes 4 to 5 servings.

⁓

Watermelon isn't just for summer anymore. Red watermelon juice, available at Central Market, makes the holiday season bright.

Texas Watermelon Sake Martini

2 ounces sake
1 ounce rum
1 ounce watermelon juice or to taste
squeeze of lime juice
watermelon wedge and mint sprig

Pour sake, rum, and watermelon and lime juices over ice in a martini shaker. Shake and strain into chilled martini glass. Garnish with watermelon wedge and mint sprig.

Makes 1 cocktail.

Making cookies using shortcut ingredients streamlines the holidays but still requires some flour to fly and emphasizes the fun part: decorating.

Shortcuts:
Texas Holiday Tricks

Remember, you have cooked if you had to wash a dish. That's my golden rule about shortcuts. And there are so many shortcuts to make life easier and less stressful during the holidays.

Many of the dishes for holiday meals—even whole meals—can be purchased as takeout from specialty markets like Central Market, a restaurant, or delivered by a caterer. That makes food preparation during the busy holidays much more manageable. But for those who love it, cooking during the holidays is as fun and meaningful as decorating, shopping, wrapping gifts, or any of the other tasks that some consider tedious and others eagerly anticipate. You may notice that Central Market is frequently credited throughout this book. That's because I can't think of any food purveyor who knows Texas culinary style any better. Central Market cooks Texas and makes it easier for all of us to eat and prepare signature dishes for Texas holidays.

With so many alternatives, you don't HAVE to cook. So pick your shots. Use this chapter to decide which shortcuts you're willing to take. Cook only what you WANT to cook: maybe it is a dish you'd like to try, one you prepare well, or something you absolutely can't buy. Don't sweat the rest. No one will care whether you bought it or cooked it as long as it's delicious.

What follow are tips and recommendations I use for making holiday meals and food gifts come together a little easier. Please add these to your repertoire. Most important: Don't feel guilty. And never—ever—apologize. Just say "thank you" when the compliments flow.

Thanksgiving Tips and Shortcuts

* Many side dishes can be made ahead and refrigerated for a day or so. Remember to add 10 to 15 minutes baking time to casseroles that have been refrigerated. To avoid breaking glass casserole dishes, remove from refrigerator 30 minutes to 1 hour before placing in hot oven.

How Do Ya Like Them Apples?
That's the name on the box that
holds this big ol' pie that looks as
dramatic as it tastes. With
4½ pounds of thinly sliced apples,
this ready-to-serve beauty is even
better gently heated through just
enough to melt a slice of cheddar
on top.

* Don't be shy about using deli or heat-and-eat sides, including macaroni and cheese, green bean casserole, or whatever else you like and fits with your menu. Same goes, of course, for desserts. Put any of these in your own serving or baking dishes. Don't look back.

* That especially goes for mashed potatoes. Warm a heat-and-eat package of mashed potatoes, and whip in some cream cheese and sour cream for a shortcut version of Really Whomped-Up Mashed Potatoes (p. 23). Can be made ahead and reheated just like the "scratch" version.

* Of course it's okay to buy cut fruit and call it Texas Ambrosia, p. 31. Throw in a few pomegranate seeds and coconut. Voilà!

* Nothing seems more tedious when gathering ingredients for a recipe than grating a tablespoon or two of citrus peel. So get this basic preparation out of the way at once. Peel and grate plenty ahead of time so you don't have to slow down when cooking. Use a potato peeler to scrape

off strips of peel from 2 oranges and 4 lemons. Don't scrape deep enough to get the bitter white pith. Use a blender or minichopper to process strips to a fine consistency or finely chop on a cutting board with a sharp knife. Store orange and lemon peel separately in resealable plastic freezer bags or rigid plastic containers. Grated or chopped peel will store in the refrigerator for a week. It will freeze for a month. Use as needed for the flavor of orange or lemon without the acidity of the juice.

* To make corn bread dressing if you don't want to bake corn bread, buy corn bread squares or muffins (frozen or from the bakery). Packaged corn bread stuffing mix works just fine as well. Guilt should not be an ingredient for the Thanksgiving meal. Or just heat and eat prepared dressing.

* To get a head start on dressing, you can crumble the corn bread and combine the sautéed vegetables with it. This may be stored in the refrigerator in a closed plastic bag or covered baking dish for several days or frozen for a month. Add stock and eggs just before baking, (see recipe, p. 17). Or you may assemble it and bake it ahead and reheat just before serving. Place in 300° oven for 30 minutes or until heated through.

* Drizzle drippings over the dressing when the turkey comes out of the oven for additional flavor.

Thawing Turkey

The best thawing how-to is usually on the turkey wrapper; some directions are specific to certain brands. However, here are a couple of generalities to get you through.

* Defrost in unopened package in refrigerator; allow 1 day for every four pounds. For faster thawing: Place turkey breast side down in cold water to cover. Change water every 30 minutes. Allow 30 minutes per pound.

* If using a fresh, never-frozen turkey, use within 48 hours of purchase. Store in refrigerator at 40°. Pay attention to "use-by" date.

Cookbook author and culinary teacher and historian Tina Wasserman credits her mother for this turkey roasting technique that was made for traveling with turkey. Cooking the turkey over a bed of vegetables keeps the meat very moist and gives you one-step side vegetables and clear gravy. Tina also offers a cooking tip for those who are kosher.

Turkey cooked this way can be made the day before and is super easy to pack and take or to reheat when guests arrive. After roasting, slice the meat and place it in a large ovenproof dish, tightly covered. Place the gravy and vegetables in separate containers. Refrigerate several hours or overnight if you plan to make it ahead. If making turkey to travel, use containers with secure lids that will stack easily in a cooler. Transport in a cooler with plenty of ice or frozen travel packs to maintain refrigerator temperature.

When ready to serve, pour some of the clear gravy over the sliced meat and reheat in the microwave according to manufacturer's instructions or place in 300° oven for 30 to 45 minutes. Reheat the vegetables and remaining gravy and serve. Your turkey will be moist and flavorful and everyone will be glad you came to dinner.

One-Step Roast Turkey, Vegetable Side Dish, and Gravy to Go

1 (10- to 14-pound) turkey, thawed completely
5 carrots, coarsely chopped
3–4 large onions, diced
3 stalks of celery, coarsely chopped
½ pound mushrooms, sliced
½ pound chicken livers, chopped (optional)*
1 (28-ounce) can crushed peeled tomatoes

---

* If you are kosher, first broil the chicken livers until almost done before dicing and adding to the vegetable mixture. Or omit chicken liver.

2–3 cloves garlic, finely chopped
salt, pepper, paprika, and garlic powder, to taste
1 tablespoon chicken fat or butter

Preheat oven to 325°. Salt the cavity of the turkey and set aside.

Place the carrots, onions, celery, mushrooms, livers, and tomatoes in the bottom of a large roasting pan. Season to taste with salt, pepper, and paprika, being light-handed with the salt if using a kosher turkey.

Place the turkey on top of the vegetables breast side up. Season the turkey all over with the salt, pepper, paprika, and garlic powder.

Rub chicken fat or butter all over the turkey skin with your hand. Use a little more fat if necessary to cover the wings and legs well. Cover with a tent of aluminum foil being sure that the SHINY SIDE faces out. Do not allow foil to touch the turkey. Leave space between turkey and foil.

Roast turkey for 15–18 minutes per pound or until the internal temperature of the breast meat is about 170° and thigh meat 180°. Baste often with the juices in the pan. If necessary, you can add some boiling water to the bottom of the pan. Remove foil for last 30 to 45 minutes of roasting to brown skin. If turkey begins to brown too fast, re-tent with foil.

Allow turkey to rest outside oven for at least 15 minutes before carving.

Remove vegetables with a slotted spoon and place in a serving dish. Pour remaining liquid into a gravy boat and serve.

Makes 8 to 12 servings.

Hanukkah Shortcuts

* What better time than Hanukkah to be celebrating in Texas where barbecue brisket is king? Instead of braising brisket, buy smoked brisket by the pound or whole from your favorite barbecue joint. Add brown gravy that you make or buy; or go Texas all the way with barbecue sauce.

- Don't forget about deli-prepared deviled eggs on a dairy Hanukkah plate.
- Make a couple of whole rotisserie chickens glamorous. Substitute them for roast chickens (p. 44) and prepare fruit as instructed in recipe, stirring in cardamom and turmeric. Bring to a boil, reduce heat, and simmer 30 minutes. May prepare ahead to this point and refrigerate until time to finish the dish. Place fruit in bottom of roasting pan. Place refrigerated roasted chickens on bed of fruit in large roasting pan. Cover loosely with foil and reheat in 300° oven 20 to 30 minutes until chickens are heated through.
- Buy it and dress it up with some seasonings or garnish: that includes applesauce, chopped liver, and latkes.
- Use frozen meatballs; reheat and top with Sweet-and-Sour Sauce (p. 41).

The tedious part of making latkes is grating fresh potatoes, even using a food processor. This recipe eliminates that step.

Shortcut Latkes

6 cups (16-ounce package) frozen shredded hash brown
  potatoes
4 tablespoons all-purpose flour or matzo meal
2 eggs, lightly beaten
3 tablespoons butter, melted, or vegetable oil
1½ teaspoons water
½ teaspoon salt, or to taste
vegetable oil as needed

Place the hash browns in a strainer; rinse with cold water until thawed. Drain thoroughly by spreading on a couple of clean dish towels. Blot with paper towels. When excess moisture has been absorbed, transfer potatoes to a large bowl.

Stir in flour or matzo meal, eggs, butter or vegetable oil, water, and salt. Mix well.

Heat ⅛ inch of oil in a large skillet over medium-high heat, about 375°. Drop batter by ⅓ cupfuls into oil. Fry 2 or 3 pancakes at a time, leaving plenty of space between each.

Flatten each pancake to uniform thickness, about 4 inches in diameter. Fry until golden brown on both sides. Turn pancakes carefully so they don't come apart and don't splatter the cook with hot oil. Drain on paper towels. Add additional oil to frying pan as needed.

To double recipe, prepare two batches of batter.

Makes 8 to 10 latkes, about 4–5 servings. See p. 46 for instructions on making latkes in advance and reheating in oven.

⁓

Refrigerated biscuits can be transformed into homemade *sufganiyot* (jelly doughnuts).

Shortcut Sufganiyot

½ cup sugar
½ teaspoon ground cinnamon
4 cup vegetable oil
1 can large refrigerated biscuits
½ cup strawberry or raspberry jam

In a bowl, combine the sugar and cinnamon; set aside.

Heat the oil in a 10-inch skillet over medium-low heat to 400°. While the oil is heating, form the doughnuts.

Separate dough into biscuits. Slice each biscuit horizontally, parallel to cutting board, to the center. Do not cut all the way through. Spoon 1 teaspoon jam into center of slit biscuit. Pinch edges of dough to seal.

Fry in hot oil until golden on each side, turning once. Drain on paper towels and coat on both sides with cinnamon sugar. Serve immediate or cool completely before packaging for gifting.

For gifting, place fresh jelly doughnuts in a tall cellophane bag and tie with blue or silver ribbon. Give them the day they're fried.

Makes 8 jelly doughnuts.

Stores like Central Market sell cook-it-yourself "kits." One Central Market "kit" I found delicious and great for Hanukkah or any other holiday meal is this Spiced Butternut Squash Carrot Soup. The ingredients come packaged together, ready to cook. Add a quart of vegetable or chicken stock.

Spiced Butternut Squash and Carrot Soup

Ingredients in kit: chipotle butter, onions, celery, butternut squash, carrots, thyme, parsley
1 quart vegetable or chicken broth
salt and pepper to taste
fresh parsley, for garnish

Spiced Butternut Squash and Carrot Soup, p. 234

Heat chipotle butter over low heat in 2-quart saucepan. Add onions and celery; sauté until onions are soft and translucent. Add butternut squash, carrots, and thyme; cook 2 to 3 minutes longer.

Add broth; raise heat to high, bringing liquid to a boil. When soup comes to a boil, lower heat and simmer, covered, until carrots are tender, about 25 minutes. Remove soup from heat; discard thyme sprig. Season to taste with salt and pepper.

Garnish with fresh parsley and serve immediately.

Makes 4 servings.

Christmas Shortcuts

* Baking cookies with children or grandchildren makes for wonderful memories and photographs. Don't let the dough be a barrier. Buy cookie dough. Buy prebaked sugar cookies. It's all about decorating with the kids. Just buy lots of frostings and sprinkles. Of course, making your own cut-out cookies with holiday-themed cutters is extra special—see the recipe on p. 98.

* Christmas Ham Shortcut: Purchase a 5-pound fully cooked boneless ham with skin and fat already trimmed. Place ham in double layer of foil (large enough to wrap ham completely) in bottom of a shallow roasting pan. Pour over ham 1 cup apple juice, cranberry juice, ginger ale, or beer. Wrap ham tightly. Place in oven and bake for 15 minutes per pound. Remove from oven and smear top with mustard and brown sugar/flour mixture; omit optional whole cloves. Return to oven, uncovered, for 30 to 35 minutes to melt and caramelize the sugar. Cool slightly before slicing and serving.

* Beef or Venison Sauce Shortcut: Use a packaged gravy such as the Knorr Hunter Mushroom and Gravy Mix or Knorr Classic Sauce Peppercorn Sauce Mix. Substitute wine for ¼ of the liquid called for and cook according to package instructions. Just before serving, stir in 1 tablespoon dry sherry or brandy or purchase

a sauce from the takeout department at supermarket, restaurant, or deli.

* Shopping for holiday treats can be as special as visiting the Christmas tree farm. Take a drive to a kolache bakery for a special breakfast or coffee treat.

* Again, holiday side dishes of many kinds, including scalloped and au gratin potatoes, are yours for reheating from deli counters or refrigerator and freezer cases. Even twice-baked potatoes.

* Instead of removing membrane and separating grapefruit into sections, cut peeled grapefruit into thin rounds, like wagon wheels. Slice wheels into half circles. Or, easiest of all, use bottled grapefruit sections from the refrigerator case.

* Never be shy about buying holiday cookies. They're beautiful, delicious, and traditional. Pass them off as your own or not.

Many holiday tables wouldn't be complete without macaroni and cheese. If there's ever a dish you don't HAVE to make this is it. There are about a zillion options from restaurant or supermarket deli takeout to frozen. Many are high quality and you and your family probably have a favorite or two. Go with what you know. If, however, you want to make mac and cheese, this is a streamlined version of old-fashioned macaroni and cheese. Not as easy as boxed, it is simpler than the classic version calling for a "scratch" cheese sauce. It'll do any momma proud.

Macaroni and Cheese

½ pound macaroni or other dry pasta
1 tablespoon butter
1 teaspoon yellow mustard
1 egg, lightly beaten
½ teaspoon salt
3 cups (about 12 ounces) grated cheddar or other
  yellow cheese (divided use)
1 tablespoon flour
1½ cups milk, or as needed

Preheat oven to 325°–350°. Grease a 1½-quart casserole.

Cook macaroni in large saucepan according to package directions. Pasta should be tender, but not too soft. Drain well and allow to cool slightly. Return to saucepan.

Stir in butter, mustard, egg, and salt. Add 2½ cups cheese and flour, tossing well to evenly distribute ingredients. Turn mixture into prepared casserole dish. Pour milk over macaroni and cheese. Use the back of a spoon to press down ingredients and level the top. Bake for about 35 minutes. Sprinkle remaining cheese on top and bake about 10 minutes longer or until the custard is set and the top is golden and crusty.

Makes 8 servings.

The key, as always, is to make a convenience product taste like it took hours to make. Here's a shortcut using canned refried beans that will make you think you've died and gone to Tex-Mex heaven. Add enough liquid and oil or lard, if you dare, to make them a silky mass, not too stiff, not too runny. And the way you like 'em.

Really Fast Refried Beans

1 cup finely chopped onion
2 tablespoons lard, bacon drippings, or vegetable oil
2 (16-ounce) cans refried beans
stock or water as needed
salt and pepper to taste

Place a medium skillet over medium-high heat. When skillet is hot, add onion and lard, bacon drippings, or oil. Lower heat and cook until onions are soft and lightly browned at the edges.

Add beans, stirring to mix well. Lower heat and cook until bubbly. Adjust texture as desired with stock or water. Season to taste with salt and pepper.

Makes 8 servings.

New Year's Shortcuts

Don't hang your head if you're all cooked out by the end of the holiday season. Go out. Take out. Hang out. Don't cook unless you want to. Use every trick you know and every convenience product you trust and love. Here are some I believe in.

* Enhanced guacamole: Combine ready-made guacamole (Central Market's is really fresh tasting) or packaged mashed avocado with 1 fresh coarsely smashed avocado and ½ cup prepared pico de gallo, or ¼ cup salsa; add salt and lemon or lime juice to taste.
* Some more favorites: Canyon Foods (or other brand) Gumbo Starter. Use opulent seafood; garnish with steamed rice and serve with hush puppies.
* Still other "bowl day" basics: Canyon Foods (or other brand) bottled chili or posole starter. Just add beef or ground turkey. Garnish with grated cheese and finely chopped onion.
* As well as prepared tortilla soup, such as Dean Fearing's, bottled by Canyon Foods. Garnish with fresh avocado.
* Canned pinto beans and black-eyed peas: canned beans are nothing to be ashamed of. Just dress 'em up. Sauté onions, garlic, ham, barbecue, and smoked or fresh pan sausage with jalapeño until onions are soft. Add to 8 cups (four 16-ounce) cans of pinto beans or black-eyed peas. Heat through and simmer for at least 30 minutes. Add cilantro or fresh thyme just before serving, if desired.
* Add a small can of chopped green chilies to ranch dressing for an easy version of the recipe on p. 123.
* For easy but authentic-tasting barbecue sauce, add 2 to 3 tablespoons barbecue pan drippings (or to taste) to 1 bottle barbecue sauce. Heat and serve.
* Frozen hush puppies will certainly do the trick with gumbo on New Year's Day.

Holiday Gifts Shortcuts

There are too many ready-made food gift options to list in this chapter. Practically any recipe for the food gifts chapter is available retail, either in a store or online. As I've said many times, pick your battles during the holiday season. Still, something homemade is even more special, even if it's the gift wrapping. If you buy it, consider personalizing store bought with your own gift basket imagination (see p. 149).

These organic chocolate truffles from Central Market are a joy. Dress them up in your own packaging, put a bow on the CM package; serve them on a dessert buffet. No need to try to pass these off as homemade. Who cares? They're great

For example, cheat a little on the homemade thing with one of the best mixes ever devised, Central Market Salted Truffle Brownies. These are an enticing combination of salty and sweet. And so good, no one will suspect you used a mix . . . unless they've also discovered this secret convenience weapon.

Below are a few carefully selected recipes for quick "homemade" gifts.

This is truly a shortcut compared to the hours of slow simmering required for Chewish Chicken Chtock, p. 168, but the result is almost as deep flavored and aromatic.

Quick and Easy Chicken Breast and Stock

1 or 2 chicken breast halves, bone in and skin on
2 cups chicken stock, plus additional water as needed
1-inch piece of ginger plus 1 clove garlic plus 1 teaspoon
   whole black peppercorns
Or
1 rib celery plus ½ onion plus 1 small carrot plus
   1 teaspoon whole black peppercorns

Place chicken into deep saucepan. Add chicken stock and additional water, if needed, to cover the chicken. Add seasoning vegetables for Asian (ginger, garlic, pepper) or European (celery, onion, carrot, pepper) flavor profile.

Place saucepan on cold burner. Turn heat to low. As the pot heats, skim the foam from the edges of the pot. Do not allow liquid to come to a full boil. It should simmer ever so gently, just so the bubbles occasionally break the surface. Cook this way for 10 minutes after liquid begins to simmer. Do not cover. Skim foam for a clear broth.

Place lid on pot, turn off heat, and steep for 20 minutes. Carefully remove hot chicken from stock and place in a large bowl to catch any drippings. Cool chicken. Strain stock to remove vegetables; discard seasonings. Strain drippings into stock. Reserve for desired use.

Meanwhile, remove and discard skin and bones. To shred the breast meat, pull small pieces of white meat in strings, going with the grain to produce strings or shreds. Or cut chicken into desired size pieces. Use for soups, salads, casseroles, nachos, enchiladas, any dish that calls for cooked chicken. You get the idea.

Makes 2 to 3 cups cubed or shredded chicken; 2½ to 3 cups chicken stock.

These are a great shortcut treat for any time of year but particularly delicious for the holidays. Mini-cupcakes are fabulous because they are the proverbial two-bite size.

Chocolate Peanut Butter Mini-Cupcakes

1 (18.25-ounce) box chocolate cake mix
1 cup buttermilk (substitute for water called for in package directions)
⅓ cup vegetable oil
4 eggs
48 mini chocolate peanut butter cups, unwrapped

Line a 24-mini-muffin pan with paper liners (or use two pans). Preheat oven to 350°.

Prepare cake batter according to package directions, substituting buttermilk for water. Follow package directions for the amount of oil in the batter. Add 4 eggs (most mixes only use 2). Beat with an electric mixer until moistened. Beat on high until batter is thick, about 2 minutes longer.

Drop about 1 tablespoon of batter into each cup of the prepared muffin pan. Place an unwrapped miniature peanut butter cup into the center of each cup, pressing down gently. Top with about a tablespoonful of batter, just enough to cover the peanut butter cup. The paper cups should be approximately ¾ full, or slightly more. Bake for 11 to 13 minutes, until cake batter is set.

Allow cupcakes to cool completely on a wire rack, about 15–20 minutes. Turn out when cool. Refill mini-muffin pan with liners. Repeat process with batter, chocolate peanut butter cups, and batter. Bake second batch.

Makes 48 mini-cupcakes.

⌒

In this case, you've pickled because you "made" pickles. What this shortcut version does is convert dills to sweet pickles. Put them in a pretty jar for gifting. No one has to know you didn't grow 'em, pick 'em, and pickle 'em from seed to jar.

Although pickling has come back into style with gardening and backyard chicken coops, it is also time- and equipment intensive. The following recipe is a shortcut version for contemporary time and tastes. Ironically, the recipe is adapted from a collection compiled in 1978 by the New Ulm, Texas, Volunteer Firemen's Auxiliary. This small German community, my mother's hometown, lies between Houston and Austin. Now, there's a place where women knew how to ride horses, bake bread, and cut up a whole chicken! They didn't take many shortcuts, and the men were darn good barbecue cooks as well.

Of course, there is a wide variety of products available in the supermarket or specialty markets, including the fine New Canaan brand from the Texas Hill Country. Their pickled green beans are particularly notable. Whether bought or homemade, pickled okra, dill pickles, sweet gherkins, bread-and-butter pickles, pickled peppers, relishes such as chow-chow, and watermelon pickles are traditional in many homes and served in Grandmother's cut-glass or crystal dishes made for these specialties.

Pickles, whether "homemade" or store-bought, make a great holiday hostess gift or a component of a Texas gift basket.

Shortcut Sweet Pickles

1 (16-ounce) jar whole dill pickles (divided use)
3 cups sugar (divided use)
1–1½ cups white vinegar (divided use)
1/3 cup pickling spice

Cut pickles into ¼-inch-thick rounds. Layer one-third of the pickle slices in the bottom of a 9 × 9-inch glass baking dish. Spread evenly with 1 cup sugar. (Pickle layer and sugar layer should be approximately the same thickness.)

Repeat layers using remaining pickles and sugar, ending with sugar. Let stand until sugar is dissolved, or about 1 hour.

Combine 1 cup vinegar and pickling spice. Pour over pickles. Add more vinegar, if needed, to cover pickles and dissolve any remaining sugar. Cover dish tightly with plastic wrap and refrigerate overnight. Pickles are then ready to eat. For longer storage, place pickles in original jar. Store in refrigerator.

Makes 4 (4-ounce) jars.

Index